The Textile

**Textile Progress
Volume 13
Number 4**

Rotor-spinning

A critical appreciation of recent developments by
C A Lawrence BSc PhD and K Z Chen BSc

Edited by P W Harrison BSc CText FTI MIInfSc

Series Editor-in-Chief P W Harrison BSc CText FTI MIInfSc

THE TEXTILE INSTITUTE

10 Blackfriars Street

Manchester M3 5DR

President: J. R. McPhee, B.Sc., D.Phil., C.Text., F.T.I.
General Secretary: R. G. Denyer, B.Sc.

Use has been made of *World Textile Abstracts,* published by the
Shirley Institute, in tracing many of the references cited in this review.

Textile Progress will be available on microfilm twelve months after publication from University Microfilms Limited, St John's Road, Tylers Green, High Wycombe, Bucks, HP10 8HR.

Printed by Stott Brothers Limited, Halifax, England

CONTENTS

TEXTILE PROGRESS

ROTOR-SPINNING

By C. A. Lawrence, B.Sc., Ph.D., and K. Z. Chen, B.Sc.

1. INTRODUCTION

This review covers the published literature and patent information on rotor-spinning during the period 1978–81. It is clear from the data reported that, apart from the effects of world-trade fluctuation, the growth of rotor-spindle installation has levelled at the 6% mark of the world's total short-staple-spindle installation. However, since the majority of the rotor-spun yarns produced are likely to be within the coarse-to-medium count range, it seems reasonable to assume that this 6% represents a very significant percentage of the total mass of spun fibre consumed and that rotor-spinning is therefore now an established manufacturing process.

The textile industry is to-day more competitive than ever, and this is taxing machinery manufacturers to produce more sophisticated, albeit expensive, machines with higher and higher production rates; and processors, in order to remain viable, are having to acquire the technology to use these machines effectively and economically. In rotor-spinning technology, this competitive edge is reflected in the implementation of faster rotor-spinning speeds, more sophisticated monitoring and control systems, and automatic start-up, doffing, cleaning, and repiecing devices. The constant requirement for a wider market area has led to research and development into the production of stronger and finer yarns, the spinning of novelty yarns, and improvement in the spinning of wool and long-staple man-made fibres. Improvements in the tribology of rotor production has resulted in quicker and cheaper replaceable components, better wear-resistant coatings on machine parts, and improved bearing life. The ergonomics of the process have also improved, to meet both health-and-safety regulations and the need to attract a more technically qualified level of staff; in western developed countries, the latter requirement is seen to have a growing significance in the economics of the rotor-spinning process.

2. ECONOMICS OF ROTOR-SPINNING

The textile industry is to-day a very cost-conscious industry; at every stage of processing, the objective is to reduce costs. Thus, the success of a new spinning process depends not only on the properties of the spun yarn but also on its economic effectiveness. Rotor-spinning, with its manifold increase in spinning speed, its lower labour requirement, and the elimination of the speedframe and winding frame, would appear to offer a very attractive proposition. The only deterring factor is its high capital cost[1].

Ripken[2] has reported the findings of a recent opinion survey – the 'Delphi Poll' – regarding the immediate-to-long-term future of the rotor-spinning process. The poll was conducted among textile-machinery builders, man-made-fibre producers, the spinning sector of the industry, and research institutes. A number of interesting points emerged. From answers to questions about the commercial and technical factors likely to limit further growth or cause a reduction in the number of installations, the economic spinning limit was held to be the most important factor. The second most significant factor was import competition from low-price countries. Of less significance were the lower flexibility of the process compared with ring-spinning and the potential competition from continuous-filament and composite yarns. The conclusion drawn, therefore, was that it is the economics of rotor-spinning that will decide its future.

In the industry, the economics are measured by the ratio of costs to performance, expressed as cost/kg of yarn. An economic comparison between alternative production techniques on the basis of unit costs is only sensible, however, if other factors in the performance are considered, i.e., that the accepted yarn quality for a particular end-use can be produced and whether or not a particular type of yarn can attract a premium sale price. In evaluating the rotor-spinning process, a comparison is always made with the ring-spinning process[3]. Owing to the fact that, in spinning over the count range of 98.4–29.5 tex (6s–20s N_e), increases in the spindle speed for the ringframe are usually higher than corresponding increases for the rotor machine, the ratio of the number of ringframes to the number of rotorframes to produce a similar yarn quality reduces significantly as the yarn becomes finer. This is reflected in the ratio of the total capital employed for the rotor system and that for the ringframe system. This ratio is 0.87 for 98.4 tex (6s N_e), reaches 1 at 59.1 tex (10s N_e), and increases to 1.36 for 29.5 tex (20s N_e). In spite of this unfavourable ratio of 1.36 for 29.5 tex (20s N_e), it is claimed that, owing to savings in labour for the open-end system, the two systems reach a point of parity at 29.5 tex (20s N_e), with a possible marginal advantage for the rotor system[3]. In situations where rotor speeds higher than 45 000 r/min are really practicable, the point of parity may extend to 24.6-tex (24s-N_e) yarns. Successful rotor-spinning is therefore still restricted at present to the coarse-count range above 25 tex (24s N_e)[1].

Production costs include capital costs, energy costs[4], and labour costs. Capital costs account for approximately 50% of the production costs. Energy costs take second place, and labour costs are the least[5].

In order to find out what effect changes in the basic parameters have on the production costs, Wulfhorst[5] investigated 23 parameters. The results are given in Tables 2.1 and 2.2 and Figures 1 and 2.

Table 2.1
Relationship between Production Costs and Parameters*

Parameter	Cost Type†						
	1	2	3	4	5	6	7
Rotor speed	×	×		×	×	×	×
Yarn twist	×	×		×	×	×	×
Machine price				×			×
Energy requirements/machine				×			
Space requirements/machine				×		×	
Wastage			×				
Direct labour costs/machine	×						
Indirect labour costs/machine		×					
Percentage maintenance of package-doffing equipment					×		
Energy requirements for air-conditioning				×			
Energy requirements for lighting				×			
Direct hourly rate	×						
Indirect hourly rate		×					
Material cost for wastage			×				
Power costs				×			
Costs per m²						×	
Capital recovery (machine)							×
Number of operating hours per annum					×	×	×

*The factors influencing production costs are listed on the left. The type of cost marked with an × (column) is directly affected by each factor (line).

†Cost types:
1 Direct labour costs
2 Indirect labour costs
3 Wastage
4 Energy costs
5 Maintenance costs
6 Space costs
7 Service of capital with respect to machine

The direct-labour requirements are affected by the following:

package weight;
package-doffing time;
can-changing time;
can weight;
piecing-up time;
number of successful piecings-up;

patrol time per spinning hour;
other downtime resulting from end-breaks;
spinning heads/machine;
incidence of yarn breakages; and
aisles.

Table 2.2
Ranking of Factors According to Their Effect on the Production Costs in the Case of Parameter Changes*

Factor	Linear Density		20 tex (N_m 50)		36 tex (N_m 28)		100 tex (N_m 10)
	R	E	R	E	R	E	
Rotor speed	− 1	1.2757	1	1.0810	1	1.1059	
Yarn twist	+ 2	0.9763	2	0.9458	2	0.8192	
Machine price	+ 3	0.5429	3	0.5480	3	0.5186	
Number of operating hours per annum	− 4	0.5025	4	0.5071	4	0.4799	
Capital-recovery factor	+ 5	0.4715	5	0.4758	5	0.4503	
Power costs	+ 6	0.2055	6	0.1859	7	0.1517	
Energy requirements	+ 7	0.1989	7	0.1794	8	0.1455	
Direct hourly rate	+ 8	0.1370	8	0.1395	6	0.1656	
Incidence of yarn breakages	+ 9	0.1078	9	0.0878	20	0.0341	
Percentage for maintenance	+10	0.0715	10	0.0721	9	0.0683	
Patrol time/spinning head	+11	0.0706	11	0.0684	21	0.0337	
Indirect hourly rate	+12	0.0592	12	0.0597	16	0.0565	
Indirect labour requirements	+13	0.0592	13	0.0597	17	0.0565	
Space requirements	+14	0.0534	14	0.0539	18	0.0510	
Cost per m²	+15	0.0496	15	0.0473	19	0.0448	
Piecing-up time	+16	0.0468	16	0.0330	22	0.0123	
Recovery factor	+17	0.0468	17	0.0330	23	0.0123	
Wastage	+18	0.0086	18	0.0195	12	0.0628	
Material cost for wastage	+19	0.0086	19	0.0195	13	0.0628	
Can weight	−20	0.0084	20	0.0193	10	0.0656	
Package weight	−21	0.0082	21	0.0189	11	0.0642	
Can-changing time	+22	0.0079	22	0.0181	14	0.0615	
Package-doffing time	+23	0.0072	23	0.0166	15	0.0565	

*$E = (\triangle K/K_0) : (\triangle P/P_0)$

$\triangle K$ = cost variation as a result of $\triangle P$ = parameter variation; K_0, P_0 = standard values of costs and parameters.
Sign − indicates falling, sign + indicates rising production costs with a rising parameter in each case.

R = ranking of factors in accordance with E values.

The factors are ranked in their sequence at 20 tex.

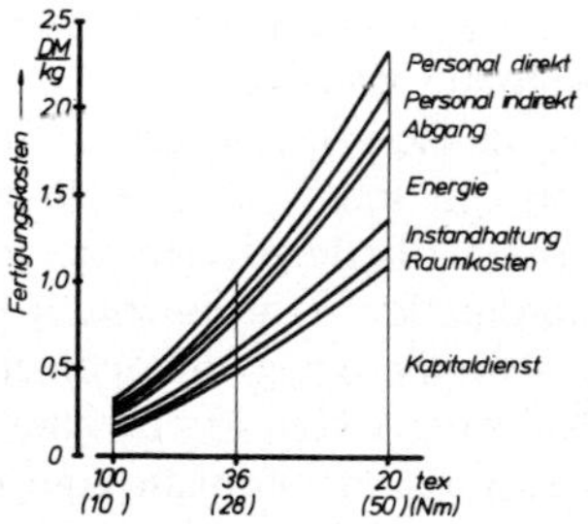

Fig. 1
Manufacturing costs of rotor-spinning, as function of yarn count: (left) manufacturing costs; (right) direct labour, indirect labour, waste, energy, maintenance, space, capital services

The results show that the rotor speed and yarn twist have a radical effect on all aspects of costs, with the exception of the costs relating to material wastage. A change in the rotor speed has the greatest effect on production costs. This is followed by yarn twist, machine price, number of operating hours per annum, and depreciation. The equation used for the analysis (see Table 2.2) is a relatively simple one, which the spinner can use to work out the rise or fall in his production costs as a result of such parameter changes as production rates, energy costs, labour costs, and the number of operating hours per annum[5].

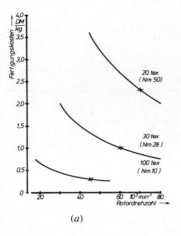
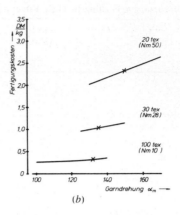

(a)   (b)

Fig. 2

Manufacturing costs of rotor-spinning as function of (*a*) rotor speed and (*b*) yarn twist at different yarn counts (apart from the abscissa, all parameters are constant; left: manufacturing costs; bottom: (*a*) rotor speed; (*b*) yarn twist)

The result of cost comparisons naturally depends on the assumptions being made[6]. These assumptions may differ considerably from mill to mill and from actual practice. The actual data regarding wages, power cost, accessories, consumption, spares, inventories, the method of calculating depreciation, repayment, and the actual interest rate may differ considerably, and it is quite possible that different economical count ranges may be obtained by different mills. In order to obtain economically the best processing conditions, the main parameters, such as the rotor speed and rotor diameter, must therefore be chosen by determining the optimal solution for a multivariate function instead of for a monadic function.

At present, two development trends can be detected in rotor-spinning machines, and these have a considerable effect on the economics of the method. They are the spinning of finer yarns and the automation of the rotor-spinning process[5].

Every automatic system increases the price of the machine but should reduce the handling times, i.e., the direct labour costs. In most cases, cost reductions achieved through staff reductions are not sufficiently large to justify the investment outlay on automatic equipment. Only if the parameters are in favour of automation is the automatic piecing-up mechanism an econmic proposition as for finer yarns and when there is a high incidence of end-breakages. The same is true of the package-doffing mechanisms, which are favourable only for coarse yarns and low package weights. In an over-all assessment of automatic equipment, consideration must be given to the pre- and post-process stages, to quality requirements, and to the unquantifiable boundary conditions[5, 7]. Improvement of yarn quality and greater package weights also contribute to improved sales opportunities and advantages in yarn-processing. The use of automation is only economical if the rotor speed can be raised by at least 10 000 r/min. The lowest costs are reached at approximately 75 000 r/min[6].

The art of successfully spinning finer open-end-spun yarns requires both technological and economic feasibility. Progress to date apparently is in the former, but it is a necessary first step in order to accomplish the latter[8]. As mentioned above, the ratio of the number of ringframes to the number of open-end-spinning machines to produce the same count of yarn is reduced as the yarn becomes finer. A prerequisite for spinning finer yarns economically is therefore spinning finer yarns at high speed on the rotor-spinning machine.

It is an accepted fact that, on an open-end-spinning machine, from 5 to 15% more twist than that used in ring-spinning has to be given to obtain a yarn that has a strength 10% lower than that of ring-spun yarn[9]. The higher twist naturally means a high rotor speed.

From an engineering viewpoint there is hardly any limitation on the upper speed range, and units can run at 100 000 r/min. Economically and technologically, it is not considered practicable for such speeds to be used, since, at this level of speed, the variations in spinning tension within the finer yarns (i.e., those of less than about 20 tex) would be equal to or greater than the strength of the yarn, so that the increased yarn breakages would not allow satisfactory commercial spinning[10]. Power consumption would increase significantly, because it increases with the third power of speed[9]. Great difficulty would be experienced in manually piecing-up broken ends. Problems with yarn-piecing and doffing of full packages can be alleviated by making the machine fully automatic and using special drives and lubrication arrangements on the machine. The main problems at this stage are the higher capital cost of such a machine and the high depreciation and interest element that would have to be built into yarn costings[10].

With increasing speed of the rotor, the yarn properties generally deteriorate. This disadvantage can be offset to some extent by using a smaller rotor diameter in spinning fine yarns at high speeds. Usually, however, a smaller-diameter rotor requires higher twist coefficients than a large-diameter rotor. As a rule, therefore, production costs cannot be reduced to the extent expected by increasing the speed of the rotor, because this makes it necessary to use higher twist coefficients, with increasing energy and maintenance costs[11, 12]. In one study, it was found that a 60% rise in rotor speed resulted in only 27% higher productivity[11]. Raising the rotor speed is therefore generally not reflected entirely in lower production costs.

3. CONTEMPORARY ROTOR MACHINES

Since the first rotor-spinning machine was introduced commercially in 1967, there has been a rapid growth in the number of makes and type of rotor machines now available. By the mid-1970s, most manufacturers of short-staple spinning equipment marketed a rotor machine within their product line. The fact that rotor-spinning is now firmly established is seen in the fact that rotor spindles now occupy 6% of the world's total spindle installations. This may seem a small percentage when viewed with the machine manufacturer's interests in mind. However, when taken in the context of yarn production, this figure represents a large percentage of the yarns spun in the coarse-to-medium count range and is therefore very significant in terms of the quantity of yarn produced. Table 3.1[13, 14] shows the total percentage increase and geographical distribution of rotor and ring spindles for the period 1974–79. It is clear that the most rapid growth in rotor installations took place during 1978–79 and at a higher rate than the growth in ring spindles for that period.

During the first fourteen years of rotor-spinning as a commercial process, several technical and technological problems were encountered, including excessive wear of machine parts and difficulties in processing some synthetic fibres and certain grades of cotton. Through the co-operative efforts of spinners, fibre producers, and machine manufacturers, modifications have been made to the machines and to the technology in general, which have alleviated many of these problems. As a result, rotor-spinning can now be considered as the most significant advancement to have occurred in high-technology spinning. There is an increasing number of automatic-piecing and package-changing devices being fitted to current rotor-spinning machines, two developments that have not had as much success in conventional ring-spinning[15]. The progress that is being achieved in this area for rotor-spinning gives credibility to the concept of a future commercially viable, fully automated spinning mill.

The rate at which rotor-spinning has grown has led to a wealth of published information on processing experience and resultant yarn properties and end-uses. In analysing the published data, a difficulty arises in that, of the number of different types of a particular make cited, e.g., the BD200 series, many have now been replaced by improved models[43–50]. However, a considerable number of technical studies reported in the literature have involved the use of older machines. It is therefore appropriate to give a brief description of the differences between the most commonly

Table 3.1
Percentage Annual Increase in Ring-spindle and Rotor Installations on a Geographical Basis, 1974–79

	Ring Spindles						Rotors					
	1974	1975	1976	1977	1978	1979	1974	1975	1976	1977	1978	1979
Africa	99.8	62.3	100	103.7	151.5	85.3	—	58.8	100	791.2	544.4	721.2
America, North	35.1	41.0	100	25.8	54.3	45.7	117.7	110.9	100	36.1	43.5	75.6
America, South	76.2	121.9	100	30.7	51.8	100.3	7.5	50.9	100	55.9	33.3	89.4
Asia and Oceania	98.3	107.7	100	59.8	90.2	144.3	52.0	32.5	100	94.3	53.7	94.9
Europe–EEC	70.4	77.0	100	51.4	46.7	54.5	33.1	64.9	100	22.6	30.3	36.7
Europe–EFTA	181.2	158.5	100	69.6	112.3	168.6	67.4	62.8	100	24.0	52.7	48.8
Europe–others	219.1	183.0	100	47.6	29.9	30.4	—	—	100	42.1	252.0	195.4
Total	99.0	102.5	100	59.0	77.1	102.6	24.7	28.8	100	52.5	157.2	140.9

Unit base: 1976 = 100.

used machine types. A comprehensive list of most makes of rotor-spinning machine is given in various publications[16, 17] and will therefore not be detailed here. However, it must be mentioned that, owing to economic forces, a number of these makes have since been withdrawn from the market.

The BD200 was the first rotor-spinning machine to be marketed, and, although it has undergone several important design modifications, the actual spinning unit has retained many of its basic initial features. It is still the only machine design that has holes machined in the rotor base to generate the required air-flow for transporting fibres to the rotor groove; as such, it is termed a 'self-pumping' rotor unit. All the reportedly more widely used models have this basic rotor design, i.e., the BD200–M69, the –M, –R, –RS, –RC, and –RCZ, and of late the –S and –SV and the future BD200BDA. However, to improve dust removal during spinning, the later models, from the –R and –RS to the –BDA, have larger and elliptically shaped holes in preference to the earlier circular holes.

Even though several other manufacturers had long since incorporated a trash-extraction box on their spinning unit, it was not until the introduction of the –RC machines (around 1975–76) that trash-extraction devices were fitted to BD200 rotor units[18]. The cleaning system differed from other makers' designs in that a number of 'plugs' or shutters were positioned within the trash-removal slot. These can be adjusted to produce a wide range of cleaning effects yet keep the unnecessary waste of spinnable fibres to a minimum, and, when a 100% synthetic fibre is being processed, the slot can be completely closed off[19]. The air intake for fibre transportation, which was formerly placed at the side of the spinning unit, is resituated at the top of the unit. This puts it within easy reach of the operative for cleaning without the necessity of opening up the spinning chamber. Thus the units can be cleaned at frequent intervals while the machine is still running[19].

The M69 model had a recommended rotor speed of 35 000 r/min, which was increased to 40 000 r/min with the introduction of the –M, –R, –RS, and –RC machines, all of which were fitted with a standard rotor diameter of 65 mm. With the –RCZ machine, the rotor diameter was reduced to 40 mm and the rotor speed increased to 50 000 r/min, the later –S model allowing speeds of up to 60 000 r/min to be used. The use of improved ball-bearing drives has extended the service life from 12 000 to 18 000 spinning hours[19, 20], and the inclusion of elastic dampers in the rotor housing has reportedly[21] lowered the noise level by up to 6 dB. Power consumption per rotor for these later machines under maximum load was also reduced to 100 W, compared with 200 W for competitive machines operating under similar conditions. The increased rotor speed would normally lead to a low manual piecing-up efficiency, especially on machine start-up, but this was offset by the fitting of a semi-automatic spinning-in system as an integral part of the machine[19]. This device reportedly gave a constant success rate of around 90% in spinning cotton with a rotor speed of 50 000–60 000 r/min[21].

Until the introduction of the –RS machine, the BD200 models were only capable of spinning fibres up to 40 mm in length[18, 22], even though the standard rotor diameter was 65 mm. The –RS was specifically designed for the production of yarns from fibres of length up to 60 mm and a maximum fineness of 3.3 dtex and involved a reshaping of the fibre-transport passage, which was made as a replaceable insert, specially coated to reduce wear caused by abrasive fibres[18]. To-day the BD200S is constructed to allow an interchange of the 40-mm and 65-mm rotors, enabling fibres of up to 60 mm in length to be spun on the same machine. Ancillary devices fitted to the machine[21, 23] include a waxing attachment[24]; a pneumatic arrangement – referred to as the 'third hand' – for producing a yarn-tail reserve on the yarn bobbins; and a wind-up provision with anti-patterning for producing either a cheese or a $3°30'$ cone package of mass 3 kg. The machine is also reported to enable a wider count range to be spun, i.e., approximately from 98 to 15 tex (from 6s to 40s N_e). Other optional features include a semi-automatic doffing carriage, which is illustrated in Fig. 3. The figure shows a leverage system, which traverses the length of the machine to remove full bobbins and replace them with empty spools from a supply cabinet that also traverses the machine. The doffed packages are placed on a conveyor, which eventually deposits the bobbins into a container pallet referred to as the APS 200 palletizing unit.

Fig. 3
Two optional features on the Investa BD200S: (left) bobbin conveyor for transporting full wound bobbins to the machine side; (right) the double-sided pneumatic mechanical system for replacing full wound bobbins by empty tubes and producing a transfer tail on the latter while the machine is running

In order to spin 100% wool and blends of wool with long-staple man-made fibres up to 120 mm, an –SV model has been marketed. The rotor speed ranges from 18 000 to 26 000 r/min, with a maximum delivery speed of 150 m/min[25]. The future model being developed by Investa is the –BDA, which is capable of operating at rotor speeds of up to 100 000 r/min. The rotors are individually driven by a low-noise-level motor, and the design of the rotor units facilitates the fitting of automatic piecing-up, cleaning, and doffing attachments. The machine is still in the development stage, and it would appear that only cotton fibres of up to 40 mm have been processed in any significant quantity. However, the machine makes it technically possible to spin finer open-end-spun yarns down to a count of 12 tex (48s N_e).

Schlafhorst's Autocoro rotor-spinning machine is one of the latest makes to enter the market and is designed to spin yarns at rotor speeds of 60 000–80 000 r/min[26–28]. The machine is equipped with a winding head, similar to that of the Autoconer, and this has helped to give it a competitive edge over many other rival makes. The building of a stable and acceptable package, particularly a cone package, has been a problem on most rotor-spinning machines, and here Schlafhorst have utilized their years of experience in the winding sector[29]. Hydraulic cradle-damping, package-cradle-weight relief, and a stable cradle, as well as anti-patterning and lateral displacement of the package edges, are all used to make a good package build-up[26]. The Autocoro therefore has a stated capability of producing quality packages, either cylindrical or up to 6° taper, as well as dye-packages. The packages produced are of 150-mm maximum traverse and of 300-mm maximum diameter. With cylindrical packages, there is a simple compensator wire to effect a tension compensation as the yarn traverses from left to right and vice versa. With tapered packages, there is a special control system to compensate for the differences between the constant delivery speed from the spinning unit and the varying take-up speed from the small to the large diameter and vice versa[29]. When a yarn break occurs, the package is automatically raised from the drum and located in a favourable position for piecing. Space has also been allowed on the winding head for the fitting of an electronic clearer and a waxing device[29].

In order to overcome the difficulty of manual piecing and package-changing at the high speeds, the Autocoro is equipped with individual autodoffing and an automatic piecing carriage[26], as shown in Fig. 4. The piecing carriage consists of a cleaning unit and a piecing unit, which operate simultaneously, so that, before every piecing operation, the rotor is automatically cleaned. A minicomputer is used to control the piecing sequence in such a way that the piecings are made, for all practical purposes, fault-free. The strength of the piecing lies within the distribution range of the normal yarn strength. Every piecing is checked electronically, and, if a piecing is not within the established tolerances, a repeat is carried out[29].

An integral-starter winding station works in conjunction with the package doffer. The system of individual automatic doffing used gives constant-length transfer tails during winding of the initial layers. The precision wind-on and the firmly fixed transfer tail are of value in subsequent processes, where automatic transfer from empty to full package is required. The

Fig. 4
The Schlafhorst Autocoro with automatic doffer

package doffer travels along the machine over the packages to place the full packages that have been removed on a conveyor and insert a new centre with an already-wound transfer tail. The piecing carriage then restarts the spinning process[27].

The spinning box was developed in collaboration with Süssen and has the familiar Süssen interchangeable rotors and noise-damped twin-disc bearings. A G-groove type of rotor is used for spinning medium counts from cotton and synthetic fibres and from their blends. For coarse yarns, an 'S-groove' rotor is recommended[27].

Schubert & Salzer's RU 11 rotor-spinning machine has a number of development changes and is now termed the RU 11 Spincomat[30]. The Spincomat is noted for joining the yarn with a fisherman's knot in place of the usual spinner's piecing[31], and the rotor bearings have been improved to allow spinning at speeds in excess of 60 000 r/min by using smaller (48-mm-diameter) rotors[32]. Each spinning unit has its own integrated automatic-rotor-cleaning device, and the cleaning action is released by the machine operator when a button is pressed (see Fig. 5). The cleaning is a pneumatically controlled action, which prevents damage to the surface of the rotor[32]. Facilities are provided for monitoring thick and thin places and moiré-producing faults and for measuring the quantity of yarn on the built package[33]. A new waxing device, which gives a more even application, has been fitted, and the wind-up system can now produce both cylindrical and conical (2°21' and 5°57') packages[34] with transfer tails[30]. The package mass has been increased to 4.5 kg[33].

The machine has a stop–start program and a package doffer for placing the yarn packages in transport trucks[30]; it is claimed that the stop–start device reduces the lost production on shift changeover or power failure. As a variant of the RU 11, the RU 80 is intended for processing

Fig. 5
Initiating automatic rotor-cleaning on the Schubert & Salzer Spincomatic (the loose end of thread is clearly visible at the top of the picture)

longer-staple fibres of up to 80 mm and is aimed at the traditional woollen and semi-worsted market for spun yarns of man-made fibres and wool and their blends. With a rotor diameter of 92 mm, the rotor-speed range is from 24 000 to 30 000 r/min for a maximum delivery speed of 150/min[33].

Rieter have developed a new Model U spinning unit for their M 1/1 machine. Its essential feature is the modified fibre feed into the rotor. This appears to be as short as possible and has involved a complete redesign of the rotor cover and feed passage. The claim is a better control of the fibres during transport to the rotor, which has made it possible to bring the yarn structure of the rotor-spun yarns more into line with that of ring-spun yarns; at the same time, the amount of twist necessary for the spinning operation has been greatly reduced[35]. It was found possible to spin cotton into 7.03-tex (84s N_e) yarn by using a twist multiplier[36] of 3.92. In addition to the modifications on the M1/1, the rotors of the new U-type units have an improved service life in excess of 20 000 hr, and it is now also possible to wind 2° conical packages as well as dyeing-packages and to wax the yarns directly during package-building. The machine further provides for the optional fitting of the Süssen automatic Spin-cat and Clean-cat devices[37].

In the long-staple sector, SACM have modified their ITG 300 open-end-spinning machine to a design primarily for spinning wool. This machine still has an apron-draft-roller opening system, which is noted for the use of a special selector roller to feed the fibres into the rotor (see Fig. 6)[25, 38–40].

Use is also made of a false-twisting device to give a low over-all real twist in the yarn, and yarns with as few as 75 fibres in the cross-section can be spun at similar mechanical twists to those used on ringframes with acceptable strength and elongation[41].

By adopting the principle of the ITG 100, the rotors are fitted on indirect bearings and are interchangeable. This allows an exact choice of diameter and type of rotor for the length of fibre to be processed[42].

Fig. 6
Close-up of selector roller on modified SACM ITG 300 machine, showing arrangement of plates to nip and not nip against rubber presser roll

The single-sided Rotospin Type 883 of Platt Saco-Lowell has been improved with the addition of a wide-gauge (210-mm) version (Fig. 7), capable of turning out larger cheese-type packages, each of mass up to 10 lb (4.5 kg). The larger packages, which are intended to reduce costs in subsequent processes, are 122% heavier than the conventional 4.5 lb (2-kg) packages produced by the regular-gauge (130-mm) Type 883 machine. The modified machine has a sidefeed into the rotor and an up-rated rotor speed of 60 000 r/min. Although the resultant yarn properties have improved, the machine has the same performance capabilities as the regular-gauge model[41]. The Rotospin Type 887, which has spinning positions on both sides, also includes the modification of the 883.

Fig. 7
Wide-gauge version of the Platt Saco-Lowell Type 883 Rotospin rotor-spinning machine

4. TECHNICAL DEVELOPMENTS OF THE ROTOR-SPINNING MACHINE

4.1 Modifications in the Design of the Spinning Unit
4.1.1 Introduction
The design of the rotor unit may be divided, according to its operation, into four sections, namely:

> *sliver delivery*, which involves interrelation between feed roller, feed plate, and opening roller;
> *fibre separation and transportation*[51], which concern the opening roller, the separation edge, and the shape and dimensions of the transport tube;

fibre deposition[51], which is dependent on the outlet of the transport tube and the rotor size and shape; and

twist insertion, controlled by the doffing-tube size and shape and the rotor-groove size and shape, as well as by their frictional properties.

4.1.2 Sliver-delivery Section

To accommodate changes in the mean fibre length, certain designs require the operative to reset the distance of the delivery-roller nip from the striking point of the opening roller. This involves either dismantling the housing to exchange certain component parts or alternatively obtaining access to adjusting screws; both techniques are too time-consuming. Figures 8 and 9 show two patented designs proposed for controlling a range of fibre lengths without major readjustments[52]. The figures show the device to consist, in principle, of two gripper elements, replacing the commonly used feed plate. The grippers may consist of either two small contract rollers (2), (20) or two sections (54), (55) of a feed block (56). The sections are machined to have a different radius of curvature when brought into position over a common feed roller (37). Three other designs[53] are illustrated in Figures 10, 11, and 12. With these, a feed funnel is associated with several delivery rollers or feed ducts, through which the sliver can be selectively fed according to the mean fibre length. In all the designs[52-55], the aim is to keep a good control on the fibres in the sliver, and there is a change from the idea of a nip point for the feed roller to a nip area over which the feed roller will accommodate a length distribution as well as changes in fibre length. With the ease of change from one gripper to another (see Figures 8 and 9, (29), (24)) or from one feed duct to another (see Fig. 12, (7), (6)), changes in mean fibre length are catered for. Although, in principle, the adjustments appear to be simple, engineering these devices would more than likely be complicated and would further increase the price of an already expensive machine.

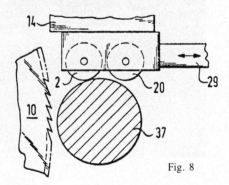

Fig. 8

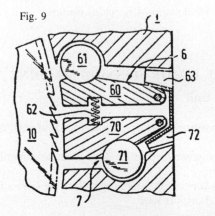

Fig. 9

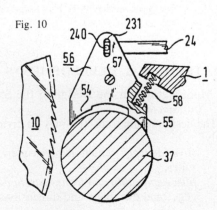

Fig. 10

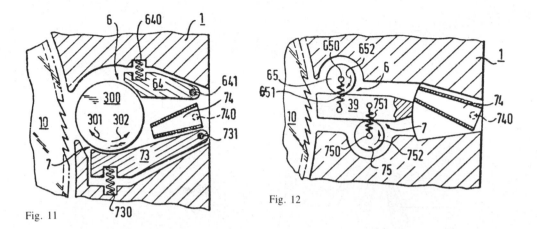

Fig. 11   Fig. 12

4.1.3   Fibre Separation and Transportation

To separate fibres from the sliver feed, the sliver is fed over a supporting surface towards the opening roller, the arrangement being similar to the taker-in region of a conventional card. Thus, to prevent damage to the fibres, the supporting surface is machined to provide a curved but wedge-shaped space in which the sliver fringe is held during separation of the fibres. Fig. 13 illustrates the arrangement; (18) represents the opening roller and (19) the machined area of the supporting surface[56]. The optimum dimensions and position of the supporting surface relative to the sliver feed roller and to the opening-roller clothing will depend on the sliver count, fibre fineness, and fibre length. Optimization of the support-surface dimensions has shown that the distances designated G and H in Fig. 13 have the main effect on yarn evenness and strength. For

$$H = (1.5 \rightarrow 2.2)\, T,$$

where T is the linear density in ktex of the sliver, and

$$G = (2.3 \rightarrow 4.2)^3\, L,$$

where L is the staple length (mm) of the fibre being processed, the resultant yarns were found to have well-above-average properties even at low opening-roller speeds. In order to effect a high degree of fibre separation, a pressing roller can be mounted on a pivotable bracket, which, through pressure from a spring, makes the roller press lightly on the land of the clothing of the rotating opening roller (see Fig. 14). When in operation, this arrangement enables the fibres in the extreme end of the sliver fringe to be separated by the opening roller.

After separation, not all the separated fibres remain attached to the opening roller. Some enter the thin layer of air (the boundary air-layer) that revolves with the opening roller. Only when all the fibres reach the separating edge of the transport tube do they leave the influence of the opening roller and enter the transport tube. Those fibres that travel in the boundary air-layer to the transport tube can readily become caught on irregular projections on the inside wall of the opening-roller housing. Accumulations of fibre can result, which are eventually removed and follow the fibre flow to the rotor to form defects in the yarn, such as slubs or neps, or cause an end-break. Figures 15 and 16[57] show two modifications of several aimed at overcoming this problem[58]. The design is for an air-stream (see arrows) to be directed down an additional inlet (12a) removing any caught fibres from the wall of the opening-roller housing. Other designs have been reported, which prevent fibres from accumulating on the roller itself[59].

Many of the irregular projections on the inside wall of the opening-roller housing result from the abrasive action of the fibres. Fig. 17 shows the use of a replaceable hard-wearing metal band

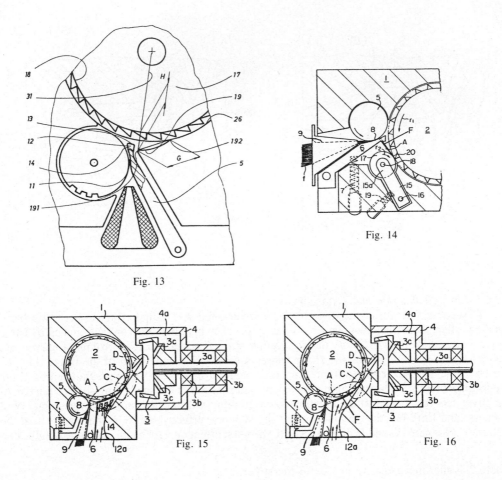

Fig. 13

Fig. 14

Fig. 15

Fig. 16

fitted in the area where the fibre makes contact with the opening-roller housing[60, 61].

Another design[62] (see Fig. 18) illustrates how the action of fibre contact with the housing can be manipulated to give better fibre alignment. By using a similar notion to the stationary-top cards, two sawtooth-wire-clothed inserts (12) and (12a) are positioned in the wall of the housing close to the opening roller. The carding action that results is presumed to give a more definite control of the fibres as they approach the transport tube. The claim is for better fibre alignment and parallelization. One important major drawback with this design is the possible 'flats-stripping effect'. Fibres are likely to become caught in the additional clothing and build up to the point where they either bring about a deterioration in the yarn properties or cause excessive end-breaks. No provisions have been made to prevent this situation from occurring.

In obtaining good fibre separation, the design of the opening-roller clothing predictably plays a major part. There are at present two kinds of clothing that are commonly used: sawtooth-wire and pinned-type clothing. A third design called a selector is fitted only on the ITG 330 machine[63, 64]. The sawtooth-wire clothing is usually wound in a helical manner around the surface of the roller drum, the drum having grooves cut into the circumferential surface to facilitate the fixing of the wire clothing. The manufacture of the wire clothing is similar to that for cards in that the tooth shape, angle, and size are cold-formed by press dies by using an already-rolled mild-steel bar[65]. After forming, the working surfaces of the clothing are usually hardened to increase their wear-resistance. For pinned rollers, the pins are made from polished

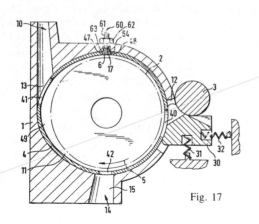

Fig. 17

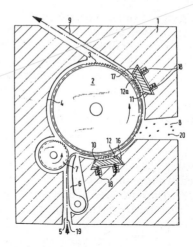

Fig. 18

hardened steel. The roller drum is made hollow, i.e. tubular, which enables the unpointed inner ends of the pins to project and almost meet in the interior of the drum[66, 67]. The pins are held in place by a cured synthetic resin[66]. Both types of roller have to be dynamically balanced; with the wire type, opening-roller portions are removed from the solid drum; with the pinned type, inert fillers may be added to the resin to give a density more comparable to that of the metal sections. These fillers can be colour-coded to indicate for which fibres the opening roller is best suited.

It has been reported that the pinned type of wire gives the better all-round effect, that is to say, better fibre separation and a longer working life. With some sawtooth-wire clothing, it has proved impossible to spin certain blends, particularly synthetic-fibre blends[68]. In other cases, it has been found that, although a yarn can be made, the distribution of the different fibres throughout the yarn is inhomogeneous. The flat land of the tooth is unable to penetrate between individual fibres or small fibre bundles of the same fibre type, which are often in the sliver after drawframe blending, and intimate mixing of the fibre types is thereby prevented[68]. The different working angles for both wire and pinned-type rollers have been well reported[69]. However, results have now shown that 60° angles, which are usually recommended for cotton, although effective in separation, give poor trash ejection and often cause trash build-up in the rotor.

The sawtooth-wire clothing is usually given a hardening treatment, but, because this can only be done after cold forming of the tooth profile, and also because a degree of ductility is required for helical winding onto the drum, the effectiveness of the treatment is poorer than for the pinned clothing[68–71]. It has, however, been found that a ceramic coating can be applied (by plasma-coating or ion-implantation) to the surface of both wire and pins to improve the resistance to wear.

In order to change the opening-roller drum rapidly without changing the bearing drive, several roller designs are available that allow the clothing section of the roller drum to be replaced by merely removing four screws. This reduces not only the operative's time taken up in changing rollers but also the cost in carrying spares, since the former practice of replacing a worn or damaged roller with a spare already fitted with new bearing drive-shafts was expensive. Further development work in this area has lead to the refitting of a base-roll component made from a plastics material. This approach offers various advantages, in that the component can be injection-moulded, which cuts the costs, and, with good quality control, the reduced weight could enable the rebalancing of the opening roller to be dispensed with[70].

4.1.4 Fibre Deposition

The fibres after separation leave the opening roller at the fibre-separating edge and flow through a duct, which, in most makes of rotor unit, opens tangentially into the rotor. The separating edge will always be subject to wear and can result in a poor fibre feed to the rotor. The fibre-feed duct generally converges towards the spinning rotor so as to limit radial movement of the fibres while in the duct. The fibres, on leaving the duct, can then be deposited onto the inner surface of the rotor in the most favourable configuration. This convergence of the duct means increasing contact between the duct and fibre as the fibre flows towards the rotor. The result can be a building up of contaminants, such as oil, lubricant and wax, and dust, in the exit area of the duct. As spinning proceeds, these deposits can result in rotor-fouling. It therefore becomes necessary to clean the exit to the fibre-feed duct periodically. This results in a longer downtime than even for rotor-cleaning. Fig. 19 shows one of a number of modifications[72, 73, 110] that allows considerable reduction in the downtime. It consists of an interchangeable ring insert, which has machined in one portion the end profile to the fibre duct (12) and is fitted in position with a locking screw (13). The downtime of the unit is kept to a minimum by replacing one ring with a spare, the replaced ring then being available for cleaning.

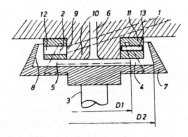

Fig. 19

The device also allows the possibility of spinning a range of fibre lengths more effectively in the same unit. As the figure illustrates, by varying the dimension of the ring insert, small- (4) and large-diameter (7) rotors can be used. The distance from the feed-duct exit to the rotor wall is critical[74]. Here a very complex, turbulent, and largely uncontrolled air-flow occurs. This will disburb the relatively well-controlled fibre orientation as the fibres leave the exit to be deposited into the rotor groove. With the interchangeable ring, this zone can be made as short as possible, which allows the leading edge of the fibres to touch the rotor wall before their trailing ends leave the duct. This also makes possible a straightening action due to the faster speed of the rotor wall[74–77].

It is claimed that the use of a tangential feed can result in greater rotor-fouling compared with designs utilizing a flanged doffing tube as a separator plate. The latter is reported to enable cleaning to be done through centrifugation of the impurities[78]. However, a tangential feed is known to produce better fibre configuration, giving better yarn strengths. Fig. 20 shows an interesting but very complicated design that allows cleaning without losing the advantages of a tangential feed[79, 80]. In the figure, (60) is the opening-roller shaft and (56) indicates the separated fibres being directed into a circular chamber. An electric field is set up in this chamber through the source (28). Dust entering the chamber will be attracted to the circular wall (20) and removed by a low-suction device (46). Highly charged points (68) and (64) are used in combination with the fibre duct to align and straighten the fibres before they travel down the duct (12) and into the rotor (8).

Work involving the fibre flow through the feed duct indicates that the fibre configuration at the outlet has a major effect on the resultant yarn properties. Studies of the configuration have resulted in the development of a number of interesting techniques for observing the movement of fibres through the feed duct, such as photographic, radio-isotope, capacitive, and photoelectric methods[81, 82]. In one paper, a holographic technique is described[83].

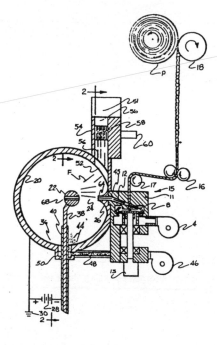

Fig. 20

4.1.5 Twist Insertion

4.1.5.1 Factors Affecting Twist Insertion The insertion of twist in rotor-spinning is influenced by the design of two machine components, namely, the doffing tube (i.e., the navel effect of the doffing tube) and the rotor (diameter and groove profile).

4.1.5.2 The Effect of the Doffing Tube on Twist Insertion Under dynamic equilibrium, the twist propagates from the navel of the doffing tube into the first 8–10 mm of the fibres collected in the rotor groove. This length of 8–10 mm of twist in the rotor groove is known as the peripheral twist extent and is important for obtaining both a good spinning performance and acceptable yarn properties[84]. It has been reported that the degree of peripheral twist present during spinning is controlled by the much-reported false-twist effect of the doffing tube[84–86]. Fig. 21 illustrates the twist distribution in the yarn as it leaves the rotor groove, passes through the doffing-tube navel, and is finally wound on the package[87]. The sudden drop in twist after the navel is an indication of the false-twist effect. If the false twist is suppressed, as in spinning with a rotating doffing tube, the peripheral twist extent is small, and a considerably higher twist factor is needed to spin without a high end-breakage rate[85]. In controlling the insertion of twist into the yarn, the doffing tube also influences the yarn structure. Results show that, as more false twist is inserted, then the more the wrapper fibres are present on the yarn surface[85]. At the navel of the doffing tube, the yarn twists back to the true twist value, which causes parts of the wrapper fibres to become untwisted in producing the final surface structure. It is, however, the degree of twist in the core of the yarn that gives the yarn its strength. Since the core fibres are those in the rotor groove, the yarn strength has been found to show good correlation with the peripheral twist extent[84]. There are two possible reasons for this. Firstly, results are given which show that the twist in the core is not always the same as that calculated from the rotor speed and yarn-delivery rate; it varies consistently with the peripheral twist. The greater the peripheral twist the higher is the twist in the yarn core. Secondly, the core of the yarn does not consist entirely (as was the view once held) of helically wound fibres, but it shows a twist difference across its diameter that is inversely proportional to the peripheral twist.

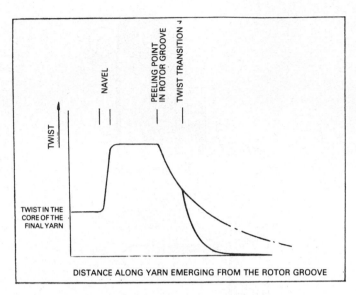

Fig. 21

Because of the relatively high tensions present within the rotor and high rotational and draw-off speeds of the yarn, wear readily occurs on the doffing-tube navel. This, of course, will influence the false twist and ultimately the yarn properties. In designing the doffing tube, two factors have therefore to be considered: control of the false-twist effect and the reduction of wear.

4.1.5.3   Control of the False-twist Effect The false twist depends upon the frictional behaviour between the yarn tail and the navel of the doffing tube and is influenced by various factors, which include the type and count of yarn, the draw-off speed, and the texture of the contact surface, as well as the atmospheric conditions. A very important factor, however, is the ratio of the yarn draw-off tension F_2, measured downstream of the doffing tube, to the calculated tension F_1 in the yarn tail between the navel of the doffing tube and the rotor wall. The tension F_2 must be greater than F_1 if spinning is to take place. However, for stable conditions, the ratio should be within the range 1.2–2.0[88]. For a given yarn count, F_1 is dependent on the rotor speed and rotor diameter and is not significantly changed by changes in doffing-tube design. The tension F_2, however, will be affected by the doffing-tube profile and frictional properties. Any such changes in doffing-tube design, in combination with F_1, will control the false-twist effect. A compromise must therefore be reached in trying to improve the false-twist effect in order not to exceed a value of 2.0 for the ratio F_2/F_1.

In altering the surface texture of the doffing tube, grooves may be cut into the navel, various ceramic coatings may be deposited on the surface of the navel, or a high degree of polishing may be used. Results have shown that there is an optimum depth of roughness for a particular fibre type and a particular yarn[88]. For example, in spinning medium- and high-tenacity polyester fibres, either in 100% form or in blends with cotton, grooves in the navel of the doffing tube are necessary. For 100% cotton and 100% low-pill polyester fibre, a highly polished navel gives the best results. With regard to yarn fineness, the finer the yarn, the smaller is the depth of roughness.

The greater the depth of roughness in the region of the navel, the higher is the false-twist effect present for twisting-in the fibres to form the yarn. However, the greater the roughness, the larger are the tension fluctuations that are transmitted to the peel-off/twist-insertion point and the greater the possible end-breaks. As a compromise between these two effects, it is necessary to vary the degree of roughness the yarn meets when drawn from the rotor groove across the navel of the doffing tube and through the exit hole in the navel. In the region nearest to the rotor groove, the depth of roughness should not exceed 0.7 μm, whereas, around the edge of the exit hole, the roughness must be less than 0.2 μm[88].

The length of yarn contact with the textured surface of the doffing-tube navel is also important for the generation of the false-twist effect. Thus, the profile of the doffing tube is as influential as its surface texture. It is reported that the contact length must be within the range 0.2–0.3 $\times$ the fibre length. Often, instead of using a new doffing-tube profile, the distance of the doffing tube from the base of the rotor can be adjusted to alter its surface contact with the yarn. In one study, on a Schubert & Salzer RU–11 machine, it was noted that an improvement in yarn properties and spinning performance was obtained by bringing the doffing tube 2 mm closer to the rotor base[89].

In practice, in spinning a range of fibre types and counts, it is necessary to interchange the doffing-tube navel. This requirement has led to several patented methods for interchanging[90, 91] and for alternative means of controlling false twist and thus reducing the downtime involved with navel interchange[92–107]. One technique is shown in Fig. 22. Here a helical wire is fitted in the exit hole of the doffing tube. The yarn being withdrawn (12) spirals around the wire and this, with the rotation of the rotor, induces the required false-twist effect and is independent of surface texture and geometry. However, piecing-up with such a device would appear to require a patient operative.

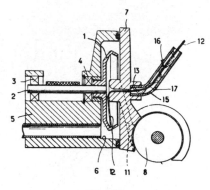

Fig. 22

4.1.5.4   Reduction in Wear The draw-off speed through the doffing tube is usually between 60 and 150 m/min, while the rotational speed of the yarn tail in contact with the doffing-tube navel is up to 80 000 r/min. On average, depending on the diameter of the navel, the rubbing speed of the yarn across the navel can be up to 1500 m/min. This can cause severe wear, quickly destroying the texture and making slight but significant modification to the profile of the doffing-tube navel[108]. The rate of wear will depend on the fibre being spun, and it is reported that synthetic fibres that are strongly pigmented, e.g., spun-dyed polyester fibre, give the fastest wear rate. Doffing tubes are usually made from mild steel, which is easily machined but has not a sufficiently high resistance to this rapid wear action. By coating the surface of the mild-steel doffing tube with a sintered aluminium oxide, the life of the component was more than doubled.

The high friction and rubbing of the yarn on the navel can also produce high-temperature spots resulting in localized melting of the fibres on the yarn surface. Increasing the wear-resistance of the component will not prevent localized melting. Patented designs have been published that incorporate a cooling system to prevent temperature build-up[109]. These systems are fairly complex and do not appear to be of practical value. In the commercial situation, the onus lies with the fibre producers, who have developed certain finishes to alleviate this problem.

4.1.5.5   The Effect of Rotor Parameters on Twist Insertion It is the compactness of the fibres in the rotor groove that both aids twist insertion, to give a good peripheral twist extent, and produces an improved yarn strength[110, 111]. Results have shown that the degree of fibre compactness in the rotor groove will depend on the rotor speed, the rotor diameter, and the tightness of the groove angle. It is now well known that stronger yarns are obtained with large-diameter rotors and a 30° V-grooved rotor, provided that the rotor speed does not produce a spinning tension greater than the yarn strength. In order to increase the degree of fibre compactness in the rotor groove, several patented designs have fitted mechanical means, which exert a controlled force on the fibre in the groove[112–115]. One such device is shown in Fig. 23[116]. The figure shows a fly-wheel (3) mounted concentrically within the rotor (8). The spindle of the fly-wheel passes down the centre of the rotor spindle, the former being driven by the pulley wheel (18a), the latter by a second (18b). The device that ensures compaction of the fibres is a pivoted wheel (19), mounted at the periphery (20) of the fly-wheel. Rotation of the fly-wheel allows centrifugal force to move the pivoted wheel in the slot (20) from position (19a) to position (19). During spinning, the fibres (fb) are therefore compressed in the rotor groove as twist runs from the yarn tail (fc) and is inserted into the fibre ring.

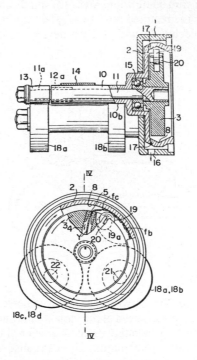

Fig. 23

The propagation of twist within the rotor groove causes the yarn to rotate on its axis while in contact with the metal of the groove. Not only does the yarn 'sweep' the surface, but it also abrades it. In the presence of the abrasive trash and dirt deposits, the high pressure between the axially twisting peel-off point of the yarn and the metal surface of the rotor groove can cause severe wear. It has been shown that the twisting torque in the groove is proportional to $W^2 R\eta \sec\psi$, where W = the rotor speed, R = the radius of the rotor groove, η = the linear density of the yarn, and ψ = the half-angle of the rotor groove[117]. In spinning low-grade cottons, at a rotor speed no greater than 45 000 r/min, this torque has been sufficient to cause complete erosion through the wall of an aluminium rotor, i.e., cutting the rotor in half at the collecting groove. Considerable efforts have therefore been made to improve the wear-resistance of the rotor surface[118–120]. These have involved the use of mild-steel rotors, but, like the doffing tube, they too suffer from wear, though not as rapidly as the aluminium rotors[118]. Several simple coatings, including nickel–phosphorus compounds applied to the aluminium rotor, have been tried with varying success[119]. The difficulty has always been to achieve uniformity of coats within the groove; for wide-angle rotor grooves (60° rotors), this technique is useful, but, for the narrow 30° rotor groove, only limited success has been achieved. It would appear from the patents that attention is being paid to plastics rotors, which can allow already-shaped ceramic inserts to be used as the rotor groove[119, 120].

4.2 Developments in Rotor Drives

4.2.1 Introduction

As increasingly higher rotor-spinning speeds become commercially realistic, machine manufactures have realized that new bearings have to be designed to meet the required low-noise, low-vibration, and acceptable-working-life specifications[121]. Present rotor-spinning machines have the design concept of a central control drive, i.e., all the rotors are driven by a common belt running the length of the machine, the driving motor and transmission mechanisms being housed at one end of the machine. However, with increasing speeds, individually driven rotors (i.e., rotors fitted to the spindles of high-frequency motors) are becoming an attractive alternative.

4.2.2 Individual Drives

4.2.2.1 Advantages Individual drives for rotor-spinning machines offer advantages regarding noise and energy, as well as a generally higher technical potential than a conventional central drive. The following are the advantages thus far observed with individual drives[122]:

    (i) noise reduction: no belt noise, fewer bearings, less air and body noise;

    (ii) reduced energy consumption: elimination of tangential belt loss, lower bearing-friction losses through elimination of bearing pressures, lower air-conditioning energy, and no loss in power factor ($\cos \phi$) in the d.c. motor;

    (iii) simplified construction: elimination of contact and energy transfer in shafts and belts, clear view of assemblies, reduced accident hazard, and great flexibility;

    (iv) improved economy: reduced maintenance, improved service access, higher production through high speeds;

    (v) improved regulation during transitions;

    (vi) higher efficiency of spinning machines, since total stoppage of the machine is avoidable in the case of maintenance and repair;

    (vii) possibilities for simplified and inexpensive operation and yarn-quality control.

As is almost always the case with engineering designs, such advantages are accompanied by equally important disadvantages. Individual drives have not yet established themselves as a commercial reality, and, before they can achieve this level of confidence, greater attention will need to be given to the factors discussed below[122].

4.2.2.2 The Cooling of Spinning Units With a central drive, the driving-motor and transmission mechanisms are housed in a section of the machine separate from the spinning units. In such an arrangement, the drives do not thermally affect the localized atmospheric spinning conditions, since the rotating parts are kept sufficiently cool by the air sucked into the interior of the rotor during spinning. With an individual drive, most of the energy at the rotor and stator surface is converted into frictional heat. The spinning conditions are therefore thermally influenced by the energy losses, since air-flow through the unit is not sufficient to cool the driving mechanisms[123]. To overcome this problem, some modified designs have an additional cooling system provided[123, 124]. The additional air-flow (the cooling air) is separated from the fibre-transporting air-flow and is conveyed into the space between the spinning rotor and the stator of an electrical motor, which thus reduces the temperature of the rotating components. With the additional cooling system, a constant temperature of 20°C can be kept within the rotor system, which is suitable for spinning most fibre types.

4.2.2.3   Accuracy of Rotational Speed Above a rotor speed of 30 000 r/min, the rotation of the rotor must be free of resonance, and the upper limiting speed is then not dictated by the drive. The maximum spinning speed is instead limited by the yarn breaking tenacity or the maximum allowable rotor temperature or both. To achieve accuracy of rotational speed, the design of the drive system must ensure a stable nominal frequency input and continuous frequency regulation[122].

4.2.2.4   Low Noise and Low Energy Consumption The noise level and the power consumption of the individual unit drives result from air friction (air noise) and bearing friction (bearing noise).

Apart from an accepted slight surface roughness of the aluminium traveller, the motor stator, consisting of individual magnets, must have a smooth surface. For this purpose, the magnets and their hysteresis ring are sprayed with a plastics coating. For the same reason, the stator must not have any open, broken-up winding. The stator winding is also sprayed with a plastics coating to produce a smooth surface. The power-savings produced by this measure amount to 10 W. A siren effect is also avoided, i.e., noise is reduced[122].

It is a known fact that a disc rotating in a free environment has greater air-friction losses than a disc enveloped by a thin air-gap in a housing. There is, however, an optimum air-gap. In order to utilize this fact, the spinning rotor should be covered with a tight-fitting rotor cap[122, 125]. The power-savings are 13 W for a 48-mm-diameter rotor at $n = 70\ 000$ r/min[122]. On the other hand, with too small a gap, there is an increase in cost because of tolerance requirements and the power consumption of the motor will also not be at a minimum. The recommended spacing is between 0.2 and 0.4 mm[123].

Bearing friction (bearing noise) primarily depends upon the sliding speed, the lubrication gap, and the viscosity of the lubricant. In order to realize high rotational speeds with low sliding speeds, the shaft diameter must be chosen to be as small as strength, capacity, and handling in manufacture and operation will allow. On the other hand, a smaller shaft diameter calls for a more viscous lubricant, to produce the desired carrying capacity[122].

In order to avoid increased friction noise through vibrations, which are the result of inherent imbalances in the spinning process, a bearing of the least possible mass must be used, and it must be elastically mounted. The elastic mountings will keep the bearing stresses within tolerable limits as the specific resonance range is passed during start-up, so that high-speed operation in supercritical r/min ranges is made possible with reasonable energy consumption. The elastic mounting also prevents noise transfer of bearing vibrations to the housing[122].

As mentioned earlier, individual drives have not yet established themselves, and there appear to be many problems still to resolve. Among them, the most important is that of the economics of individual drives, because each spinning unit must be equipped with an electric motor. If the benefits obtained as a result of using the individual drive cannot offset the increased capital cost, then this method is unlikely to reach commercial operation.

4.2.3   Central Drive

4.2.3.1   Advantages and Disadvantages Most central-drive systems utilize a common tangential belt-drive arrangement. This drive is cheaper and more simple than the individual-drive system. However, in order to operate at high speeds, the problems of vibration, high temperature, noise, and wear have also to be resolved. The solution lies primarily in the improvement of the rotor bearings.

4.2.3.2   The Ball-bearing System Reported improvements in the ball-bearing system were obtained by using elastically mounted arrangements similar to that shown in Fig. 24[126, 127]. Resiliently yieldable rings (6, 7a, 8a, 19a) are sandwiched by a bearing casing and a holder so that any vibration can be absorbed. The modulus, the number, the size, and the sucuring positions can be arbitrarily changed as the operational conditions, such as the rotational speed of the rotor, are changed. At least two such rings, spaced apart along the axis of the spindle, should be disposed between the bearing casing (19) and the holder (5) and at least one (8b) or (13) detachably secured to the bearing casing[126, 127]. The elastically mounted bearing gives high reliability in operation, reduces the noisiness of the machine, and eliminates the negative effect of oscillation on the other parts of the spinning unit[128].

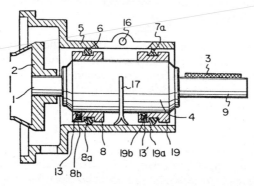

Fig. 24

The high temperature generated in the rotor area will shorten the life of the anti-friction bearings and also that of the resilient support members of the bearing arrangement. In order to cool a bearing arrangement of the type shown in Fig. 24 with maximum efficiency and the lowest possible cost, a heat-conductive body of high thermal conductivity, made in the form of a sleeve, was positioned between the bearing casing and the rotor housing (see Fig. 25)[129]. As the figure shows (A–E), a number of thermally efficient profiles can be used to effect good heat transfer from the bearing casing to the rotor housing. Fig. 26 shows that a finned design to the outer bottom surface of the rotor base (15) can be used to give extra cooling of the bearing casing[130]. Further cooling can also be obtained with the oil-feed device (18). The device includes a reservoir, which is responsive to reduced pressure caused by rotation of the spinning shaft. Thus no oil is supplied when the shaft is stopped. However, during operation, the bearings are kept reasonably cool while being lubricated.

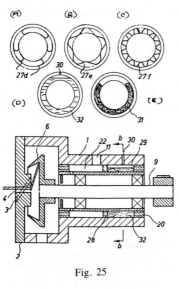

Fig. 25

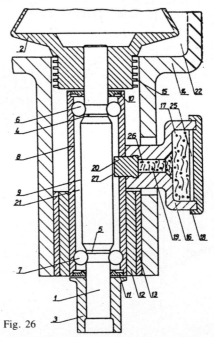

Fig. 26

With current rotor speeds of up to 60 000 r/min, rotors fitted with ball-bearing drives are operating at the practical limit for such a drive system[131]. Thus, with the constant development aimed at achieving faster and faster rotor spinning speeds, air-bearings have become an attractive alternative, particularly because of their low power consumption[132].

4.2.4 Air-bearings

At present, air-bearings are not in wide usage, although the constraints in using them are not so much economic as technical. This is because of the difficulties in ensuring the high machine tolerances, the fear of breakdown during long running times, and the high rates of air consumption[131]. Several reported modifications[131, 133] have been made to reduce the air consumption to acceptable levels[131, 133].

4.2.5 Indirect-bearing Drives

A second alternative to using direct-bearing drives is the use of indirect-bearing drives, and, because the technology is simpler than that of air-bearings and facilitates certain operational advantages (i.e., replacement of spinning components such as the rotor), some machinery manufacturers have already opted for this system[134–136]. The majority of commercial open-end-spinning machines capable of spinning at a rotor speed of 100 000 r/min utilize indirect-bearing drives. In this system, the shaft of the rotor is driven by a tangential belt and rests in a cradle formed by four supporting discs, (3), (4), (5) and (6), as shown in Fig. 27. The discs act as the bearings for the rotor shaft and are themselves fitted with direct ball-bearing drives (7) and (8). The outer circumference of each disc is fitted with a synthetic-fibre ring, which acts as a damper to give vibration-free running of the rotor[137]. The complete system is then supported on an elastic base as one block to prevent any problems due to rocking motions at right angles to the rotor shaft[138]. It would appear, from the number of patented design modifications, that the elastic support block *en masse* had not totally solved the problem[138–142]. The rotor shaft is itself subjected to a twisting–rocking motion, resulting from the relationship between the tangential belt drive and pivot points on the disc, the result being constant deflexions of the rotor shaft from the true axis of rotation. Figures 28–31 show several of the patented modifications to ensure a stable axial location. In Figures 27[139] and 28[143], sections are machined into the rotor shaft (2g in Fig. 27; 2c in Fig. 28) to provide a precise location of the shaft and therefore a true axial rotation.

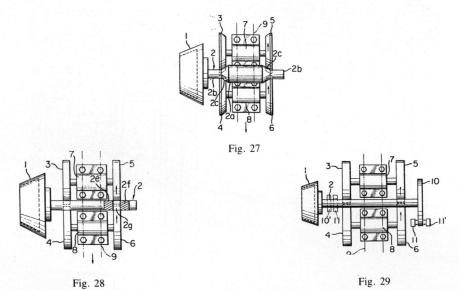

Fig. 27

Fig. 28

Fig. 29

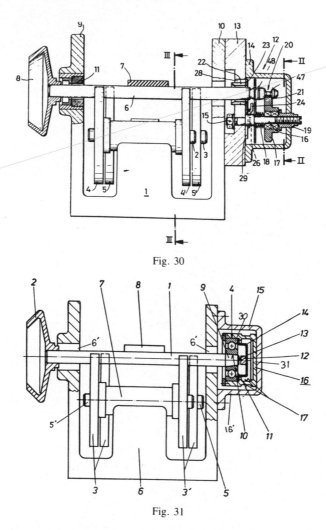

Fig. 30

Fig. 31

The remaining figures illustrate the use of shaft end-arrangements to obtain the same effect. In Fig. 29, a permanent disc-shaped magnet (10) is fitted on the rotor shaft at the opposite end to the rotor. A pair of permanent magnets (11) and (11′) are spaced at a predetermined distance to allow (10) to revolve between them. Since they are of the same polarity as (10), the tendency will be to keep the magnetic disc constantly in a central plane and hence maintain the rotor shaft in a fixed axial position. Fig. 30 shows the rear end of the shaft to extend outwardly through the rear wall of the bearing block[144]. A rotatable disc (17) is attached to the rear wall and is positioned to locate into an annular T-slot cut in the end of the rotor shaft, which maintains the precise running of the disc in the T-slot and ensures the axial location of the shaft within the supporting rollers 4–4′ and 5–5′. Fig. 31[145] is a variation of Fig. 30; in preference to the disc, the shaft end is tapered and fitted in a tapered hole of a roller bearing.

A completely new approach to the problems of indirect-bearing drives is illustrated in Fig. 32[146, 147]. Here three tapered rollers, (4), (5), (6), are positioned in a housing (9) with their axes forming a tetrahedron to support a shortened tapered rotor shaft. The shaft is driven by the tapered roller (4), which is connected through a ball-bearing drive (10) to an electric motor (11). The advantage of this arrangement is that the full length of the rotor shaft is in contact with the rotating discs, and this will ensure a constant axial location.

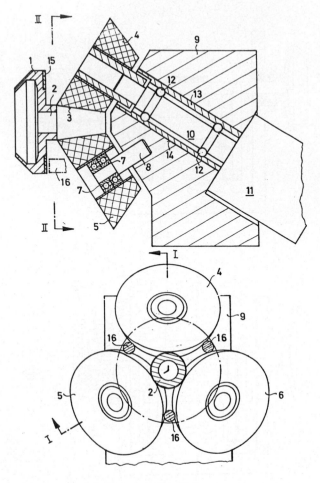

Fig. 32

4.3 Yarn-monitoring

4.3.1 Introduction

A considerable amount of work has been done to reduce rotor contamination; improvements have been made in the entire fibre-to-yarn area – from the cultivation of the cotton to its harvesting, from ginning to the cardroom, and, in particular, from carding to the individual parts of the rotor-spinning machine. The success of these efforts is much in evidence, for example, in the development of efficient equipment designed to undertake preventive measures, such as the periodic cleaning of the rotors. These efforts have helped to improve the quality of rotor-spun yarns and ultimately to reduce the incidence of fabric defects, such as moiré patterning. Nevertheless, the incidence of such defects is still too high, and additional methods for preventing their occurrence are required. A precise analysis of the moiré effect has shown that the associated periodically occurring defects in the yarn lie in the area where measured thick places, which usually occur in conjunction with a thin place, are a disturbing factor only in their periodicity and not in their size. The size of a thick place is about 8–10% of the average yarn count, with lengths ranging from 5 to 10 mm[148]. In order to prevent individual spinning units from producing such defective yarn on a rotor bobbin, it is recommended that the yarn be continuously monitored.

When such a periodic disturbance occurs, it can be detected and removed, either manually or with a programmed autocleaner or doffer.

There are two types of monitoring system being marketed, namely:

(i) an individual monitoring system, i.e., attached to each rotor unit; and

(ii) a mobile monitoring system.

4.3.2 Individual Monitoring System

In this system, every spinning unit has a detector, which is designed to measure continuously either the yarn diameter or the spinning tension.

In order to detect periodic faults in the yarn, it is necessary to convey the signal generated by the detector through electric filters[149], which are adjusted to the expected frequency of these faults, termed the moiré frequency, f_0. The moiré frequency can be calculated according to the following equation[148]:

$$f_0 = \frac{V_0}{\pi \phi},$$

where V_0 is the withdrawal speed and ϕ is the rotor diameter.

Since the delivery speed of the yarn is a variable, it is possible to use either narrow-band filters, which are more sensitive because of their variable midband frequency, but consequently more expensive, or very wide-band filters, which cover the range of delivery speeds. It is true that, in the latter case, the costs for the circuits are lower, but the wide-band nature of the filters means that a considerable proportion of the frequencies corresponding to the irregularities in the spun yarn can pass undetected. A moiré effect is therefore only detected, when wide-band filters are used, if it stands out very distinctly from the normal irregularity of the thread[150]. One reported method for overcoming this limitation subjects the yarn signal to pulse-shaping, after which the shaped pulse train is integrated and compared with a predetermined threshold value[151]. The range of yarn counts that can be monitored is extended as a result of the fact that the processing of the thread signal is kept independent of the thread-delivery speed.

One well-reported commercially available unit based on the continuous measurement of the yarn diameter is the Peyer–Turocon monitor[152–154]. The system identifies yarn faults by registering the fault and pre-selecting the desired thresholds on a control unit. The spinning station is automatically shut down if the registered yarn fault exceeds the threshold[154].

The signal-evaluation system used in the Peyer–Turocon monitor carries out a continuous frequency analysis of the yarn signal. This is performed over a frequency band of from −5% to +5% of the moiré-defect frequency. By limiting the frequency analysis to the band width from −5% to +5% of the moiré frequency, one can achieve a good separation of the periodic moiré signal from the simultaneously existing normal yarn irregularity.

In utilizing the spinning tension for monitoring the yarn irregularity during open-end spinning, it is in essence the difference between the centrifugal force acting in the rotor on a defective length of yarn and that acting on a perfect length. Each measured value is compared with a predetermined threshold value so that a defective length can be registered and removed when this threshold value is reached or exceeded[155]. FMK Mfg Ltd manufactures an electronic multi-point tension-monitoring system based on this principle that has the trade name Tenscan. Tenscan contains a solid-state transducer unit, which can be fitted to any yarn-processing machine. The Tenscan system is entirely electronic and is now claimed to perform three primary functions[156]:

(i) it sequentially measures in groups of four positions the tension value of each yarn emerging from the spinning unit by an individual solid-state transducer, which reads the tension continuously over a pre-set measuring period;

(ii) it compares the tension measured on each position with the pre-set limit; and

(iii) it indicates on a data-logger display the location of each position found to be outside the permitted-deviation limits.

Other methods of individual rotor-monitoring have been studied but have not yet reached commercial viability. One such method is to monitor the radial deflexions experienced by the rotor or its bearing. The method is suitable for an open-end-spinning system having an elastically mounted rotor or having a rotor mounted in a floating bearing. For these rotors, even limited deposits of dirt in the rotor will give rise to an imbalance, i.e., the axis of inertia no longer coincides with the rest position of the rotor axis[157]. A sensor can therefore be arranged to sense any radial deflexions experienced by the rotor or its bearing and the associated signal related to the occurrence of yarn irregularities. Irregularities above a certain size or of a periodic nature can be made to emit a signal to a display or to switch off the spinning rotor or to perform both functions[157–159].

If individual motor drives are fitted to the rotor machine, the current consumption of each motor can be used to monitor the yarn irregularity[160–162]. To recognize the incidence of slubs and flaws or structural changes (or both) in the yarn, a sensor device located to respond to changes in the current flow to the motor is provided. As with the previously mentioned system, if the changes in the value of the measured factor (in this case, the current) exceeds a pre-selected value, an electric signal is generated, which flashes a warning light or shuts off the rotor drive.

4.3.3 Mobile Monitoring System

The proposed use of a mobile monitoring system is to offset the relatively high capital outlay associated with individual monitoring arrangements[163]. With the mobile-monitoring approach, a carriage is fitted to the spinning machine with a sensing device (or devices) of the type used for individual monitoring. The carriage can be programmed to monitor each position consecutively for a given time interval or to monitor units giving a sample of the production selectively. The carriage can be made to stop the rotor unit or mark individual rotor units where the running quality of yarn is below that required.

4.4 Stop–Start Mechanism
4.4.1 Desirable Features

The stop–start mechanism, as the name implies, is used for controlling the stopping and starting operations of all the units on the rotor-spinning machine at the same time. This is particularly useful for shift changes and power failures.

In terminating the spinning operation on a rotor-spinning machine, it is desirable to stop the machine so that, at all the spinning positions, the end of yarn is not withdrawn from the doffing tube but terminates at a predetermined position and has the desired tail shape. These features are required so that, on restarting the machine, successful piecing-up is achieved at all the spinning positions and the yarn piecings have the desired strength[164]. Most of the latest models of rotor-spinning machines will be found to have a stop–start mechanism. Although there are variations between one manufacturer's device and another's, their basic stop-and-start procedures are similar.

4.4.2 The Stop Procedure

In the stop procedure, the sliver-feed rollers and the yarn-delivery rollers decelerate in synchronism. A detector, monitoring the speed of the yarn-delivery rollers, will, immediately a predetermined speed is reached, initiate the stopping of the feed rollers. After a further few seconds, determined by a time-delay circuit, the decelerating yarn-delivery rollers are braked; the rollers come almost to rest before they are braked[164]. Finally, the drive to all the spinning rotors is switched off, and the drive to the traverse guide is also switched off. The tension on the yarn between the delivery rollers, the traverse guide, and the yarn-wind-up drum is maintained[165]. It is important to note that the delivery rollers and wind-up drum are stopped at a time when the yarn end, resulting from the break in the sliver feed, still remains in the doffing tube under the suction effect of the partial vacuum in the spinning rotor[166]. Because the yarn end will be given a strong twist, this suction must be sufficient to prevent the yarn end from snarling after the rotor stops and thereby shrinking upwards out of the doffing tube.

In order to ensure that the yarn end remains in the doffing tube, a yarn-holding device can be used to keep the yarn end in the rotor until the residual twist causing snarling falls off; the yarn end can then remain in the doffing tube under the suction present in the rotor[166]. On starting, the yarn end is not released by the device until the suction in the spinning rotor reaches substantially the same value as that present during normal spinning operations. This results in a greatly increased success rate in yarn-piecing on restarting the spinning machine[166].

4.4.3 The Start Procedure

On starting, all the spinning rotors begin rotating simultaneously; the yarn-take-up rollers are then rotated in the reverse direction to push the yarn ends down the doffing tubes and into the spinning rotors. The yarn end is next attached to the ring of fibres left in the rotor groove during the stop procedure[167]. As soon as the ring of fibres begin to be peeled from the rotor groove, the sliver-feed rollers are set in motion[168], the take-up rollers are reversed to their correct direction of rotation, and the spinning process begins. Because of the high spinning speeds involved, this sequence of operations has to be performed within fractions of a second. However, because of the considerable mass and moment of inertia of the take-up rollers and the bobbin winding-up drums, instantaneous start-up at delivery speeds is practically impossible. To prevent shearing of the drive shaft during start-up, the initial speed of the take-up system is comparatively slow, and so too is the reversal to the correct spinning direction. Once the yarn is pieced up, the delivery rollers and winding-up drum accelerate to their actual pre-selected spinning speeds[169].

In order to ensure a successful piecing within the fraction of second in which the yarn end enters the rotor and is removed again, the speed of the rotor at the instant at which piecing-up occurs must be lower than the actual rotor-spinning speed. In other words, the twist at piecing-up must be comparable to the spinning twist. Thus, because the delivery speed is less at start-up, the rotor speed must also be proportionally lower than the normal spinning speed. This requirement of a lower rotor speed presents a problem in that the fibres in the collecting groove must experience a certain centrifugal force in order to be sufficiently compact for twist to propagate into the rotor groove. As one solution to the problem, the rotor is initially accelerated to a speed N_2, twice the value of the speed required for piecing-up, N_1 (see Fig. 33). The rotor speed is then rapidly decreased until it falls within the lower-speed region, $N_2 - N_1$, in which yarn-piecing can be effected. Thereafter, the speed of the spinning rotor is increased to the required spinning speed, N_0. During rotation of the rotor at N_2, a sufficient vacuum is produced in the rotor to stretch the yarn end and prevent it from being snarled. If a large package is present on the machine at the time of starting-up, then another problem can arise. A large inertia force will be imposed on the yarn package because of the quantity of yarn on the package, and slip can occur between the package and wind-up roller at start-up. Owing to this slip, the tension on the yarn is increased between the package and the nip point of the delivery rollers, so that a yarn break can occur in this area. Naturally, such a yarn break renders the yarn-piecing-up operation difficult at the start of the spinning-in cycle. Again, owing to the slip, when the direction of the winding-up drum is reversed to the true spinning direction, reversal of the package direction will occur a second or so later. Accordingly, the timing of drawing out the yarn from the spinning rotor is upset, and the number of successful yarn-piecings is remarkably reduced. In order to alleviate this effect and enhance the ratio of success in the yarn-piecing operation, the drives to the sliver-feed roller, the winding-up drum, and the delivery rollers are all operated at an optimum timing sequence for the established spinning conditions. The optimum timing sequence is determined from the amount of yarn wound on the yarn package during normal spinning. Thus, the quantity of yarn wound on the yarn package is detected at a time just before the machine is stopped. The time for complete stoppage of the winding drum is set on the basis of the quantity of yarn on the package. As a result, the delay in stopping the winding-up rollers after the delivery rollers is greater the larger the quantity of yarn on the yarn package. In starting-up, this time delay is also used. Consequently, the possible yarn breakage and mis-piecing owing to a slip are prevented[170]. As a further aid to ensure an adequate twist level for piecing-up during the start-up of the machine, several devices can be attached to the start-up mechanism[171, 172].

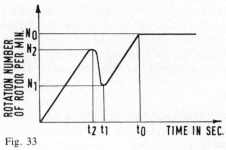

Fig. 33

The automatic starting and stopping of the rotor machine are effected by controlling different motors, clutches, and brakes according to a so-called stop–start programme, i.e., the delay-timing sequences. On high-speed modern machines, such complicated control functions are performed by electronic control units, which can also perform additional auxiliary functions, such as determining the quantity of yarn produced, monitoring the vacuum in the rotor, and monitoring the electrical voltage. However, care has to be exercised in using such equipment, since vibrations, humidity, electrical disturbances, faults in the material, and inappropriate handling can cause premature failures[173, 174].

4.5 Automation of the Rotor-spinning Machine

4.5.1 The Need for Automation

One of the objectives of open-end-spinning research and development has been to develop fully automated systems for rotor-spinning machines in order to increase production. Automation of the rotor-spinning machine must include automatic piecing-up after an end-break during spinning, automatic cleaning of the rotors when cleaning is required, and automatic doffing of the full yarn packages.

The necessity for automation stems from technical, economic, and social factors[175]. The technical factors can be summarized as follows:

    (i) a productivity increase;

    (ii) quality improvement and quality assurance;

    (iii) the future-oriented-machine concept,

and the economic arguments are:

    (a) compared with the ring-spinning frame and the manually operated rotor-spinning frame, the automatic machine, under present-day conditions, produces yarn more economically up to a count of c. 20 tex (N_e 30); Fig. 34[176] shows the production-cost comparisons for 1 kg of yarn from ring-spinning, manual rotor-spinning and automatic rotor-spinning;

    (b) if account is taken of the future increases in labour costs and further developments in the productivity of the automatic rotor-spinning frame, then the economic viability of automation should increase year by year;

    (c) automation offers the possibility to activate capacity reserves currently under-utilized (e.g., operation over the week-end).

These are unique arguments in favour of the automatic rotor-spinning machine, even if, in certain countries, the spinning costs are at present at the same level as those of competing systems[175].

As a machine, the rotor-spinning frame is best suited, owing to the application of the latest construction experience, to fulfil the demands for reduction of noise and dust levels. If successful operation of an automatic rotor-spinning frame can be achieved with a greatly reduced work force during the night shift, a further contribution to amenable working conditions can be realized[175]. The advantages for the social and human aspect therefore become self-evident.

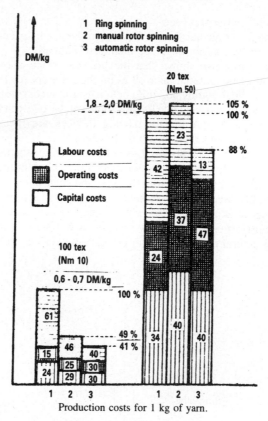

Production costs for 1 kg of yarn.

Fig. 34

4.5.2 Developments in Automatic Piecing-up

In order to increase the productivity of the rotor-spinning machine substantially, the rotor must run more quickly, i.e., in excess of 60 000 r/min. This, of course, does not just mean that only the rotor speed has to be increased. Associated with higher rotor speeds are[177]:

a higher take-up rate, which can be up to 200 m/min;

a higher fibre throughput via the opening roller; and

a shorter dwell time for the yarn in the rotor.

An important condition for running at high rotor speeds is that it is still possible to make piecings[177] while meeting the requirements relating to the quality of piecings, which are:

an adequate strength (at least 80% of the yarn strength);

an adequate extension; and

a low variation in mass (i.e., in thick places a mass no higher than + 100% compared with the over-all yarn mass).

In one study, it was concluded that the optimum strength of the pieced-up section is very strongly influenced by the accuracy with which the requisite number of fibres in the yarn cross-section is initially fed into the rotor, both too many and too few resulting in a weak piecing[177]. Too many fibres will produce a thick piecing with a twist level lower than the set twist level, and too few will give a thin piecing with a high twist level.

By measuring the fractions of a second for which the feed roller supplies fibres to the rotor before piecing commences for a number of currently used commercial rotor speeds, it was found that the optimum piecing strengths were obtained after the following times:

for 45 000 min^{-1}: after 0.55 sec;

for 55 000 min^{-1}: after 0.45 sec; and

for 67 000 min^{-1}: after 0.33 sec.

This means that the feed time has to be reduced at higher rotor speeds, and thus a situation is reached at which piecing-up can no longer be managed manually.

Practical experience has also shown that the limit at which manual piecing is possible depends on the yarn count and material, as well as on the rotor speed. However, at speeds over 60 000 r/min, manual piecing is hardly possible, or at least the success rate is drastically reduced. The piecings that do occur are unacceptable in appearance and too low in strength for trouble-free post-spinning processing[175, 177]. Automatic-piecing devices are therefore needed on rotor-spinning machines for speeds in excess of 60 000 r/min.

Automatic piecing-up at present involves one of two systems: the individual system and the travelling system[178]. In the individual system, the mechanism used for piecing-up is fitted to each spinning unit (see Fig. 35)[178]. Piecing-up with this system can be done on each unit separately, or on all units in one assembly. Because of the rapid reactions of the servo-automatic mechanism, it is possible to piece-up at almost the full rotor speed. Each unit is activated by central electronic-control circuitry. For a fault in the system, it is possible to replace the faulty part immediately; even the central control unit can be exchanged. This reduces production losses during a breakdown.

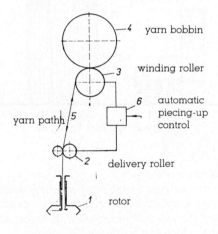

Fig. 35

Fig. 36 shows diagrammatically the travelling type of device[178]. The mechanism used for piecing-up is positioned outside the delivery rollers and the normal package-winding units and travels around one or more machines. This means that, when an end breaks, an individual spinning unit has to wait until its position in the patrol route is reached before being pieced-up, which, of course, loses production time. Any fault in the mechanism of the travelling system results in a considerable loss in production time because the mechanism itself has to be removed from the machine. A reserve device has therefore to be used, since it is impossible to replace any of the mechanisms in the travelling system quickly because of lack of accessibility and the handling of its considerable weight. The use of a reserve device, however, increases the cost.

A comparative study of both systems showed that individual piecing-up was more advantageous than the travelling system[178]. With the individual system, the production losses did not exceed 0.25%, whereas, with the travelling system, losses can be from 0.15 to 20.7%. However, the capital costs for fitting individual units to each spinning position are likely to far exceed those of the travelling system.

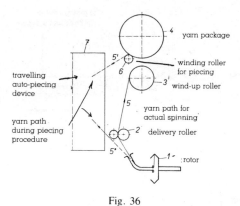

Fig. 36

4.5.3 Further Development Work

When a yarn break occurs, the sliver feed has to be stopped and the rotating package braked. With increasingly higher production rates, the stoppage of the fibre supply to the spinning rotor needs to be carried out as quickly as possible. If this interruption in the feed is too slow, then an overflow of fibres into the rotor will occur and will clog the rotor. With rotor speeds in excess of 45 000 r/min, clogging of the rotor presents a fire hazard, owing to the frictional heat generated by the fibres being rubbed against the rotor casing. To alleviate this problem, several new sensing devices have been developed to replace the spring-loaded trip-wire switches commonly used on present commercial machines to detect yarn breaks and switch off the feed-roller drive[179–181]. Improved braking arrangements have also been designed for stopping the drives to the feed rollers, the delivery rollers, and the wind-up drum[182].

The fibre feed required for producing the ring of fibres for the piecing operation depends not only on the manner of restarting the feed but also, to a considerable extent, on the condition of the sliver fringe offered to the opening roller. In open-end spinning, the fibre length has less significance with respect to the strength of the yarn than it has in ring-spinning. Thus, shortened fibres present relatively little problem. On the other hand, short fibres permit the ring to be broken with less trouble, which improves the appearance and quality of the yarn-piecing. During piecing, irregularities can result from bridging fibres, i.e., wrapper fibres. These are more pronounced when longer fibres are present. The sliver feed therefore needs to be performed in two stages, i.e., with the shortened fibres fed first and followed by longer fibres. To accomplish this, the opening roller, in combination with a compressed-air supply, serves as a means for parting the two lengths, the compressed air acting on the sliver fringe before the opening roller and removing the short fibres before the opening roller removes the larger lengths[183, 184].

In the rejoining of a broken yarn, several operations are required, namely, cleaning the rotor, locating the end of the broken yarn on the spool, returning the yarn to the doffing-tube outlet, reinserting the yarn into the rotor, starting the feed, and reinserting the yarn between the delivery rollers. These operations are carried out as the rotor is accelerated up to its spinning speed[185]. Fig. 37 shows control of the automatic-piecing sequence[176]. Among the operations, two are particularly delicate, namely, conveying the yarn to the doffing-tube outlet and reinserting it into the rotor so that the end of the yarn attaches itself to the fibres in the rotor groove. The success and quality of the joint depend on this latter operation[186]. Basically, there exist three methods of conveying the yarn to the doffing-tube outlet. For one method, the piecing-up device has a yarn-locating head (e.g., a hook), which locates the broken end of the yarn on the package while a friction roller drives the package[187]. The device also has guides for determining its trajectory (Fig. 37) between the position of the package on the wind-up drum and the position at which the retrieved yarn end is inserted into the doffing-tube outlet[188].

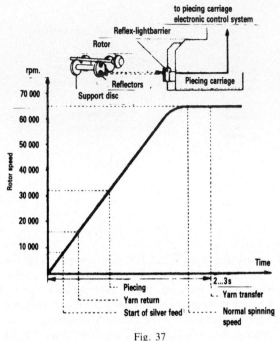

Fig. 37
Control of the automatic-piecing sequence

In a second method, the piecing-up device includes a two-arm suction tube with a suction nozzle. The suction tube is mounted on a pivot, which enables it to scan the package for the yarn end. The yarn end appears to be transferred from one arm to the other when being inserted into the doffing-tube outlet[189, 190].

A third method consists in the yarn end's being returned from the package (17) via the wind-up drum and delivery rollers (16), (15) (see Fig. 38), which are switched to a reversed motion. The yarn end enters the spinning rotor (19) through a withdrawal chamber (6). When piecing-up occurs, the delivery rollers are switched to their forward motion, and spinning recommences[191-196].

As mentioned earlier, timing has a crucial effect on the quality of piecing-up. This means that automatic piecing-up does not always produce good pieced-up sections with the requisite quality criteria. It has to be 'programmed' to obtain the maximum success rate.

In order to control the process and particularly the operation of feeding in the fibre and drawing off the yarn, the rotor-spinning machine should be provided with a pulse generator, to generate pulses proportional to the rotor speed, the generator being connected to a control-circuit box. The preliminary feed to the rotor of the number of fibres required for the piecing operation, the return to the rotor of the yarn end to be pieced, and the removal of the yarn from the rotor during its acceleration up to speed can all then be automatically timed. The advantages of the generated-pulse system reside in the facts that the nature and quality of the piecing position are adapted as accurately as possible to the nature and quality of the spun yarn and that neither the piecing aparatus nor the control unit will generally have to be readapted or reset if the operating speed of the rotor is altered or if the fibre being processed or count being spun is changed[197-200].

The pulse can be produced by means of a photo-electric cell operated by suitable reflective markings applied to the surface of at least one spinning rotor, a high pulse frequency being obtained from a large number of markings. The pulses are processed into control signals with counters or multipliers or both[198].

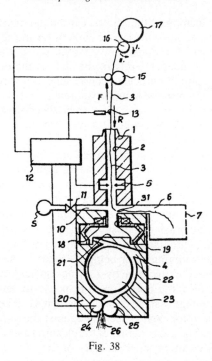

Fig. 38

To further ensure an acceptable yarn-piecing, control of the rotor acceleration up to spinning speed should be provided so as to lengthen the time in which the piecing steps can be performed. A non-contact electromagnet or electric-eddy-current braking can be provided for countering the driving torque to the rotors. The result is a flattening of the acceleration curve and a lengthening of the time period for piecing[201–203].

In order to prevent or reduce the formation of loops and kinking in the yarn during the acceleration phase after the initial piecing, due to the difference in the inertia of the spool and the thread and feed rollers, the piecing device should control the course of the yarn between the feed rollers and the spool. The driving mechanism for the wind-up drum should also be adjusted to ensure a correspondingly rapid acceleration because of the greater inertia of the drum compared with the delivery rollers. A yarn-tensioning means for maintaining constant yarn tension can also be included[204].

When the yarn package is driven at a greater speed in the normal winding direction, the pieced end is returned under tension to the yarn guide. The winding speed of the package is then restored to its normal value. For conical packages, the tension is maintained only when a special length store is provided[205].

The traversing of the yarn by the traverse guide should therefore not begin before the pieced joint is wound on the cheese, since otherwise a yarn break could occur and would be considered a failure of the automatic-piecing operation[206].

In order to maintain a standard quality of piecing, a device for monitoring the yarn can be used. A data logger is provided for storing the information concerning the number of successful piecing operations at respective spinning units or machines[207–215].

4.5.4 Automatic Cleaning of the Rotors

It is now well known that, as the running time of the spinning unit of an open-end-spinning machine increases, the rotor becomes fouled, and the quality of the spun yarn deteriorates. Cleaning of the spinning rotor is therefore of importance not only in relation to the properties of yarns but also for obtaining a good piecing after an end-break, since otherwise the piecing-up operation will fail[216]. If the cleaning of the rotor is carried out manually, the degree of cleaning and the ultimate success in piecing will depend largely on the thoroughness and skill of the operating personnel. However, for consistently well-cleaned rotors, automatic cleaning is needed, which can be effected independently of the skill of the operating personnel.

If an interruption in the spinning process occurs, such as a yarn break or the doffing of full yarn packages, it is necessary to remove from the spinning rotor the fibrous ribbon and the yarn end that have been sucked into the rotor after the yarn has been severed. Besides this, in order to confine the rotor-soiling within certain limits, it is recommended that the spinning rotor should from time to time be stopped and cleaned[217].

Cleaning of the spinning rotor can be carried out by two methods: mechanically and pneumatically. In the mechanical method, the cleaning elements are usually rotary brushes. A mobile service device includes the cleaning brushes, having a diameter smaller than the open side of the spinning rotor to be cleaned, a drive motor for rotatably driving the cleaning brush around its support shaft, and a selectively movable lever mechanism for moving the brush into and out of the spinning rotor. The cleaning brush and its support shaft are carried by a crank mechanism for moving the shaft and brush in a circular motion so as to ensure engagement of the brush with the yarn-collecting groove in the spinning rotor being cleaned[218]. Another arrangement is for the cleaning brushes to be connected to the drive by a spring-loaded lever, which gives the brushes a radial movement during the cleaning operation in response to centrifugal forces[219]. With this arrangement, there is the advantage that the cleaning elements can be pressed with sufficient force against the inner walls of the rotor, and especially against the yarn-collecting groove, without danger of damage to the rotor. The adjustability of the cleaning elements radially with reference to the rotor axis further allows cleaning independently of the rotor diameter and shape[219, 220].

With the pneumatic method, compressed air is used for cleaning the spinning rotors[221-225]. In one arrangement, the spinning rotor is moved from its normal operating position to one in which a nozzle can direct a pressurized air-stream towards the sliding surface and collecting groove of the rotor[221].

In an alternative arrangement, the rotor is rotated at a speed less than the spinning speed[223]. A first flow of cleaning air is directed to the collecting groove of the rotor, and a second flow of cleaning air is simultaneously directed to the periphery of the rotor at an angle different from the first. At least one of the flows of air is directed in a pulsating manner. The air-flows can be supplied through ducts machined into the cover plate of the rotor housing. It is claimed that in this way not only is satisfactory loosening of the trash from the rotor wall achieved, but, even with the rotor not stationary, positive removal of the detached trash also occurs[223].

In order to produce a deliberate interruption in the spinning to enable the rotor to be cleaned, a yarn monitor should be positioned so that, on measuring a fall-off in the yarn properties, it switches off the sliver-feed roller. Alternatively, to ensure that the length of yarn leaving the rotor after the break does not contain the fault, the yarn itself can be broken[226, 227]. In this case, a mechanical device slackens off the yarn tension in the vicinity of the monitoring sensor sufficiently for a cut to be made in the yarn and ultimately interrupt the supply of fibres to the rotor.

4.5.5 Automatic Doffing of Full Yarn Packages

One of the most difficult tasks of the operative (usually female) is undoubtedly the doffing of full open-end-spun yarn packages, which are situated above the rotor in nearly all makes of machine. It requires a degree of skill and physical strength, especially if the mass of the full yarn package exceeds 1 kg, and this applies to all bobbins whose width exceeds 85 mm. Moreover, it is important to replace full bobbins by empty tubes safely while the machine is running, without interrupting the spinning process[228, 229].

In order to reduce the physical and mental exertion of the operative, automatic doffing of full open-end-spun yarn packages has been developed. There are two systems: semi-automatic and fully automatic.

For the semi-automatic system, a supply station is fixed at each spinning unit for storing a supply of empty spool tubes already wound with starter yarns. A travelling servicing carriage is guided on tracks adjacent to the spinning units and has lever mechanisms for effecting the removal of a full bobbin and its replacement with an empty spool tube at each supply station. Package-changing with this system means repiecing the yarn. Each supply station is filled manually while the travelling servicing carriage is automatically driven to effect the tube-transfer operation[230].

In the fully automatic system, doffing is performed without interrupting the spinning process. While the full package is being removed and replaced with an empty one, the running end of yarn passes through a suction tube into the machine's waste-collection system. After the empty spool tube is in place, the running yarn is returned to the tube, where a transfer-tail is wound before releasing the yarn to the regular winding traverse. Doffing without interruption of spinning has the advantage that there is no loss in production (apart from the small amount lost during the doffing cycle); the spinning position does not stand idle while it waits for the subsequent piece-up operation[231].

On removal by the automatic doffer, the packages are placed on a conveyor extending the length of the spinning machine. A second conveyor is positioned between the first conveyor and a container, which ultimately receives the packages. This second conveyor is driven at a higher speed than the first to allow the packages to be automatically stacked in columns in the container[232–234].

On the whole, the fully automatic doffing system greatly reduces the effort of the operative's job and in saving labour increases the number of machines per operative. The net result is an improvement in the working conditions and a possible reduction in production costs.

5. TECHNOLOGICAL DEVELOPMENTS IN THE SPINNING AND PROCESSING OF ROTOR-SPUN YARN

5.1 Trash Removal

5.1.1 Introduction

In the early days of rotor-spinning, yarn manufacturers were attracted by the potential of the process to reduce raw-material costs by utilizing low-grade cottons and waste. To-day, although it is accepted that such raw material can be processed, it is also recognized that greater attention has to be paid to the resultant yarn quality and, consequently, the cleanliness of the sliver feed. Contaminants in the feed material present rotor-spinning with a special problem that does not exist in ring-spinning.

5.1.2 The Effects of Trash on Rotor-spinning

Trash (micro-dust in particular) will accumulate in the spinning-rotor groove during spinning. Work by Nield and Abadeer[235, 236] has shown that particles of dust and trash find their way into the bottom of the rotor groove during spinning, despite the fact that the groove is continuously occupied by the fibre ring. These particles cannot actually penetrate the fibre ring, and many are absorbed into it and thus carried forward with the yarn. However, it is possible for particles to by-pass the fibre ring in the following way. Firstly, the ring tapers from a maximum cross-section at the peeling point to virtually zero just behind it. Secondly, the surface of the slide wall is continually exposed to a varying degree as the yarn arm revolves relative to the rotor, and this permits the deposition of particles on the slide wall. Rotation of the yarn arm in the peripheral-twist zone works such deposits down the slide wall and into the bottom of the rotor groove. A thin film of dust then forms over the rotor surface and subsequently coalesces into small blobs of material appearing at random points in the groove and acting as nuclei for further deposits. These deposits may sometimes become detached or displaced round the groove, but usually they increase in length, thickness, and weight until they merge to form a complete ring.

Spinning can continue for a considerable time after the ring has formed but becomes difficult when the ring reaches a certain thickness (2.2 mm)[236]. The progressive accumulation of such dust particles interferes with the process of yarn formation in the rotor and causes a gradual change in yarn appearance and a decline in yarn properties. Eventually, the process of yarn formation is interrupted altogether, and the end breaks. The time to reach this stage is regarded as the 'maximum spinning time'[236].

Lord[237] pointed out that the yarns have not only variations in linear density but also significant variations in twist density. As the peeling point approaches the embedded particle, twist cannot propagate within the rotor groove. Once the peeling point passes over the twist trap, the twist propagates in a more normal manner. Thus the twist level of the material in the rotor groove varies cyclically. The maximum twist level at the peeling point is considerably greater than that of the yarn wound on the package because of the false-twist effect of the doffing tube. Untwisted fibres are continuously added to the already twisted 'core' in the rotor groove, and the complex structure is then partly untwisted as the yarn passes through the navel. Thus, with the added effect of trash, there are periodic portions of yarn with little or no surface twist and others with high twist. This will give yarns of widely differing appearance, which may occur side by side in the fabric and cause an objectionable fault or 'bar' in the cloth. If a single large particle of trash becomes lodged in the rotor, the consequent regularly recurring fault in the yarn causes the familiar 'moiré' diamond-patterning effect in the cloth[238]. Another comparison of yarn spun on the same unit with clean and completely fouled rotors showed no differences in yarn irregularity and nep count. But the yarn structure, which was defined by the values of the relative twist difference and tenacity, did depend on the degree of rotor-fouling[239].

Owing to the high end-breakages concurrent with rotor-fouling, spinning can become impracticable[240]. However, it must be pointed out that not all end-breaks are caused by dust and trashy substances accumulating inside the rotor. Coll-Tortosa *et al.* [238, 239] report the results of a large-scale analysis of end-breaks in an open-end-spinning mill:

> 'The end-breaks occurred mainly because of disturbances in the yarn-formation process in the rotor groove. The most important causes were the formation of tufts (31.5% of breaks); dirt or 'fly' accumulating at the trash-removal slot and then being drawn into the rotor (28.5%); impurities in drawframe sliver, which should have been removed during opening and carding (24%); only the remaining 16% of breaks was attributed to the deposits of dust in the rotor.'

Over half the end-breaks recorded were caused by faults on the machine. Problems for which the machine is to be blamed include slub formation and the intake of trash accumulations from the trash-extraction point. On modern rotor-spinning machines, such faults have been eliminated in part by appropriate modifications to certain components.

Huber[241] reports that the chemical composition of the trash and dust present in the baled cotton, as well as the levels, varies with the type and grade of cotton; and that, in processing the raw cotton, the different properties of the impurities must be considered. Only by selective treatment for each type of impurity can effective cleaning be obtained.

Analysis of the particle contaminants that give poor spinning performance has resulted in the following general classification[242–249].

> *Coarse trash:* particles that are larger than 500 μm. These include husk, stalk, leaf, and seed fragments.
> *Dust particles:* contaminants between 50 and 500 μm in size. As well as fine fragments of seed and leaf particles, dust particles contain a high percentage of fibre fragments.
> *Micro-dust:* particles between 1 and 50 μm in size.

The chemical composition of the micro-dust particles has received most study. This is because observations have shown that it is the tendency of the micro-dust particles to coalesce that presents the problem. Chemically, micro-dust consists of 50–80% cellulose, mainly in the form of very fine leaf and fibre fragments. The remainder is a mixture of mineral (quartz and clay) particles and waxy, greasy substances[250].

Several studies[251–253] have shown that the coarse visible trash is relatively loosely held between the fibres and can therefore be removed by conventional cleaning equipment. The dust particles are partly loose and partly attached to the fibres and, with the improvement in modern cleaning lines, can also be removed effectively in the blowroom and at the card. Micro-dust would appear to require a completely different cleaning action. The micro-dust particles that are tightly held on the fibre surface, possibly by electrostatic charges, can only be loosened by the fibre-to-fibre rubbing action produced at the drawframe[253]. Since up to 80% of the micro-dust particles are cellulosic, it is reasonable to assume that these are fibre fragments resulting from the intensive cleaning action in the blowroom and that more gentle opening and cleaning, as well as dust extraction during carding and drawing, would alleviate the problem. Over the last ten years, development work has therefore involved studies to improve gin-cleaning so as to reduce the need for a high degree of intensive action in the blowroom, as well as studies of the removal of dust at the card and at the drawframe, and also at the rotor-spinning unit itself.

5.1.3 Dedusting at the Gin

The effectiveness of gin-type lint cleaners for improving the cleanliness of raw cotton was studied by Towery and Baker[254]. An increased licker-in speed and combing ratio and reduced batt weight were found to improve cleaning efficiency but only slightly to reduce the degree of rotor-fouling. At a constant batt weight, an increase in licker-in (saw-cylinder) speed and combing ratio reduced the rotor residue by about 9%. However, at a constant combing ratio, increases in licker-in speed together with corresponding decreases in batt weight had no significant effect on the turbine residue. At a constant licker-in speed of 107 r/sec, an increase in combing ratio from 25.0 to 34.7 decreased the residue by about 7%, which suggested the possibility that the combing ratio has more effect on the turbine residue than the licker-in speed[254].

The use of abnormal amounts of lint-cleaning at the gin in combination with maximum mill cleaning, although decreasing the cardroom-dust levels, did not provide adequate reductions in the airborne-dust level. If one adds to this the loss of staple length ($\frac{1}{32}$ in., i.e., 0.79 mm), together with the accompanying lowered yarn strength (break factor), the conclusion is that the use of cotton fibres as a competitive textile raw material is likely to be destroyed by multiple-stage lint-cleaning before the allowable level in the cardroom is attained[255].

5.1.4 Dedusting in the Blowroom

The blowroom has seen significant developments directed towards more efficient opening and dust removal for rotor-spinning[256, 257].

In principle, a typical machine inventory for a modern blowroom[258] could consist of:
  a bale opener;
  an opener/pre-cleaner (e.g., a mono-cylinder cleaner or Axi-flo opener);
  an automatic blender (e.g., Aeromixer, Multi-mixer);
  two intensive opener/cleaners (e.g., ERMI and ERMII or Air-jet cleaner); and
  a fine opener/cleaner/chute-feed distributor (e.g., flock feeder).

Despite a large material throughput, the blowroom must separate a considerable part of the trash from the good fibres and remove it, very good results being secured if so-called mini-tufts are produced in the early part of the opening stage. Opening into very small tufts is advantageous because a large part of the trash content will then lie on the surface of these tufts. By repeated beating of the fibre tufts between the cylinder and the outer casing, the trash particles detach themselves and are separated from the system via grid bars[258].

Stepwise dust extraction often parallels the cleaning operations by all blowroom machinery removing the dust where it is generated. These removal points result from the air-handling in the blowroom and bring about a substantial reduction in the dust content[258].

Special dedusting devices may be installed additionally at suitable points between the blowroom machines. For example, after delivery from the two intensive cleaners, dedusting condensers can be fitted to dedust the material just opened, up to 60% of the micro-dust being removed. The same function, but without involving the use of moving parts, is performed by a dust extractor, which can be fitted straight into the transfer ducts at various points and takes up little space[258].

The over-all cleaning efficiency for most conventional blowrooms lies between 60 and 70%[258]. Where modern machinery is not installed, the addition of two intensive cleaners can raise the room-cleaning efficiency from just over 60% to 76.3 and 78.6%[257, 258]. The mean fibre length is, however, shortened with the heightened cleaning and the proportion of short fibres (those less than 12 mm long) increased[258].

For the rotor-spinning machine without fitted trash boxes, extra cleaning in the opening room slightly reduces the rotor-trash accumulation; however, improved carding conditions can give better results. For the machine with fitted trash boxes, extra blowroom cleaning has no value[257].

5.1.5 Dedusting on the Card

After its treatment in the blowroom, the material cannot yet be regarded as adequately cleaned. Consequently, the card must supplement the blowroom by separating short fibres, impurities, and dust. The ideal feed sliver for open-end spinning is one whose fibres are straight, clean, and well separated[259]. Thus, among the preparatory processes, particular attention should be paid to the card[260, 261], which is suitable for removing both dust and trash, as well as for achieving good fibre separation[262]. The combination of dirty cotton and good carding produces a superior spinning performance to that achieved with clean cotton and poor carding. In other words, better processing can, to a certain extent, offset the deficiencies of the input material[263]. The old saying 'Well carded is half spun' applies with even greater accuracy to the rotor-spinning process[264].

There have been several improvements in high-production carding, directed towards increasing its cleaning power. Crushrolls are, of course, essential, but it is important that the crushroll pressure be correctly adjusted to suit the grade of cotton being processed and uniformly distributed across the width of the card. It is also essential that the doffer web should not be unduly thick: crushrolls cannot operate effectively with a web of mass/unit area greater than about 6 g/m^2, and the optimum web mass is about 4 g/m^2. It is an often-expressed opinion that the use of crushrolls may tend to break the larger pieces of trash into too may particles and so inhibit the effectiveness of the trash eliminator on rotor-spinning frames and increase rotor deposits. Kirschner has shown that, contrary to the above viewpoint, the use of the crushrolls reduced rotor deposits on the Schubert & Salzer RU 11 rotor spinner (with trash extractor) by 37.3%. With the Elitex BD200R rotor spinner (without trash extractor), crushrolls reduced rotor deposits by 28.1% and were also found to improve the yarn appearance. Crushrolls actually enhance the efficiency of operation of the rotor-unit trash eliminator in two ways:

(i) by reducing the size of the very large trash particles, which might be prevented from being ejected at the separation edge by the dense 'screen' of fibre in the air-stream; and

(ii) by enabling the trash eliminator to operate more selectively and economically; because some spinnable fibre is usually attached to pieces of seed coat, the elimination of the trash particles also involves the loss of spinnable fibre, but crushing the trash frees the fibre from the seed coat, which facilitates their separation at the trash box[264].

Other successful improvements in the carding process have been the adoption of efficient dust hoods and card-waste collection systems[265], modified under screens, additional carding rollers in the feed region of the card, and exhaust apertures (or slots) cut in one or other of the card plates. These measures have enhanced the cleaning power of the single card, but their effectiveness in reducing rotor deposits is not as significant in comparison with the performance of the tandem-carding system[264].

With the 'first-generation' rotor spinners (those not equipped with trash-elimination devices), it was generally found that acceptable levels of operating efficiency, breakage rate, etc., could only be achieved by using tandem-carded sliver. More modern rotor spinners, although operating adequately with single-carded sliver, do so more efficiently and produce significantly better yarns when spinning sliver from tandem cards. This is not only because tandem-carding is very much more efficient than single-carding in removing trash and microdust, but also because the tandem card achieves the ultimate degree of fibre individualization[264].

The second card of the tandem – called the 'finisher' card – receives from the first card – the 'breaker' card – a fine web of fibre in which the cotton tufts have already been substantially separated, and which has been passed through a web-purifier crushroll. The finisher card therefore has the ideal conditions for completing the process of fibre separation and trash or microdust removal. The breaker card has relatively coarse settings and card clothing, whereas there are very fine settings and a close point population on the finisher card. This facilitates a relatively gentle and progressive carding action, so that fibre breakage and waste loss are normally lower on tandems than on single high-production cards[264].

The advantages of tandem-carding are as follows:
  (i) the tandem card can remove more trash than the single card, which enables the rotor-spinning performance to be maintained over longer periods[266];
  (ii) the tandem-card route can give the better yarn properties[267];
  (iii) the tandem card can lead to maximum operational efficiency of the very costly rotor-spinning machines; and
  (iv) the tandem card can lead to a higher production rate, at least 35% higher than that of a high-production single card[264].

In discussing the improvement of cards for sliver preparation for rotor-spinning, it is appropriate also to consider the merits of autolevelling at either the card or the drawframe. It is the general consensus of opinion that long-term autolevelling (LTAL) should be carried out at the card, to enable the autolevelled sliver to receive the maximum degree of doubling at the drawframe. A fundamental characteristic of all LTAL systems is to give good correction for long-wavelength variation in mass, i.e., > 140 m, at the expense of short-wavelength variations. The latter can, however, be corrected during drawing by doubling. This long-term regulation at the card and doubling at the drawframe become complementary in function. In cases where waste or very short fibres are to be processed it is also recommended to fit a short-term autoleveller (STAL) at the card and so dispense with drawframe doubling. (see Fig. 39)[264, 268]. Drawing of this type of feed material is difficult and uneconomic. STALs operate by varying the draft applied to the sliver at the card delivery rolls. This enables regulation of up to a wavelength of 1 m to be achieved, and the sliver can be spun directly from the card.

Technically speaking, autolevelling should be applied as near the end-product as possible. At the same time, economy demands that the number of autolevellers used should be as few as possible. Thus, there is an argument for LTALs to be used at the drawframe rather than at the card. Again, however, the inadequacy of LTALs to correct short-term variations necessitates that they are used only at the first passage of drawing.

Published data have shown that autolevelling can assist in making significant reductions in end-breakage rates, largely owing to the more than 50% reduction in count variation, e.g., from 3.5% to less than 2%[269].

5.1.6 Dedusting at the Drawframe

During drafting, fibres are displaced longitudinally in relation to each other, and the attendant frictional action loosens any dust particle adhering to the fibre surface. A suitably applied suction device can, then, remove a substantial amount of the liberated dust[270]. Studies of the efficiency of dust removal at the drawframe have indicated that up to 90% of the liberated dust can be removed if suction is applied at the top and bottom rollers of the drafting zones and that a further improvement is obtained if suction is also applied at the sliver trumpet[271]. By using a Platt

Fig. 39 (*a*)
Close-up of Crosrol-Varga Mk 3 DU dual-delivery carding system showing STAL short-term autolevellers

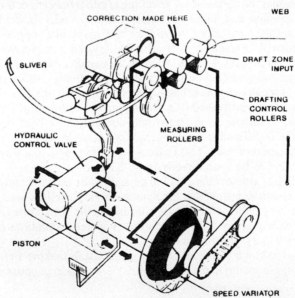

Fig. 39 (*b*)
Schematic diagram of STAL short-term autoleveller

Saco-Lowell 3-over-4 Versamatic drawframe fitted with a variable vacuum-cleaning system, it was found that, after two drawframe passages, the degree of rotor-fouling on an Elitex BD200M rotor spinner was reduced by 30%[272]. Other reported results show that rotor-fouling can be reduced by up to 40% with suction applied at the drawframe[273].

    If the drawframe is to be utilized for dedusting the sliver feed, it is essential to fit a flow control that can be varied to increase the rate of air-flow according to increased sliver weight or production speeds or both[271]. It is also important that exhausted air is not discharged straight into the workroom, since very fine dust can pass through the filter cloth of the machine and accompany the air back into the room. The exhaust duct should be coupled with the ducts of the cards and piped into the controlled filter plant before the air is recycled[270].

Even with improved cleaning and dedusting at the card, and dedusting at the drawframe, the sliver will still contain an appreciable amount of impurities. How much this residual trash-and-dust content of the sliver affects the spinning performance depends on the remnant quantity and on whether a trash-removal device is fitted to the rotor units[270, 274]. Published recommendations for the maximum acceptable level of remnant trash vary. Plekhanov[275] reports that, for the BD200M69 machine, spinning 25-tex yarn:

(a) the maximum level of residual foreign matter should not exceed 3.5%;
(b) the content of hard trash in the residual should be less than 0.4%, i.e., 4 mg/g of sliver;
(c) each particle of trash must not be heavier than 0.15 mg; and
(d) soft impurities must be lighter than 150 mg.

These recommendations appear to be applicable only in spinning yarns within the region of 25 tex. Other tests have shown that, from 0.15% residual trash, the degree of rotor-fouling severely affects the spinning performance[270].

In spinning cotton blends, the question of which rotor machine may be used is decided primarily by the trash content of the sliver. The irregular quality of the finished yarn determines the upper limit for the trash content with a particular spinning system. This limitation is dictated by the deposits in the spinning rotors[270, 276].

5.1.7 Improved Cleaning at the Rotor Unit

5.1.7.1 Limitations of Trash-extraction Devices Ten years ago, rotor units without trash-extraction devices underwent strong competition from units with such facilities, even though the latter were more costly. To-day, trash-removal systems are available on all makes of machine, but, with the growing awareness of the relation between rotor cleanliness and unit cost (i.e., manual cleaning, auto-cleaning, down-time, etc.), work is still focussed on this area of rotor development and has resulted in several patented designs.

Trash-extraction devices found in present-day rotor machines are subject to three limitations, as follows.

(i) They can remove only coarse-particle trash effectively. The troublesome 'micro-dust' particles are so small that they are hardly affected by the centrifugal forces (generated by the revolving opening roller), which present trash-removal systems are designed to utilize. These particles therefore remain in the air-stream and pass by the removal device into the rotor with the fibres. If there is a high rate of flow of fibres past the device, due to the spinning of coarse counts or high production speeds, larger trash particles may also be prevented from leaving the fibre flow to the rotor.
(ii) If the feed sliver contains tufts or bundles of fibres, these are unlikely to be fully broken down into individual fibres, so any trash trapped in the fibre bundle will enter the rotor groove.
(iii) The trash-removal device tends to disrupt the smooth flow of fibres to the rotor, and accumulations of short fibres can build-up at the separation edge, where they eventually hinder the passage of trash to the collection box.

From the available patents, it would appear that efforts are being made to improve the present systems by:

(a) modifying the design of the trash-collection box; and
(b) making alterations to the suction system connected to the box.

5.1.7.2 The Trash Box Figures 40 and 41, respectively, show that the opening-roller clothing (12) and (23) can have a right-hand or a left-hand spiral winding when fitted to the roller drum[277]. In either case, trash that is ejected can rebound back into the path of the fibre flow and travel onto the rotor groove. What is required is for the trash particles either to enter directly into the trash box (10) or to do so after deflecting from the wall (8) or (9) of the box. Once in the trash box, the trash can be sucked away via the exit (11). If a high suction rate is used, there is a reduced chance of the trash particles rebounding back into the fibre flow. However, increased suction can result in fibres also being removed from the flight path to the rotor. Fig. 42[278] illustrates one approach of many[279, 280] for improving the system. The broken lines represent the trajectory of the trash particles. Increased air-suction is provided for by an additional inlet (14), positioned away from the fibre flow. Although this design alleviates the problem of rotor-fouling by rebounding trash particles, it does not appear an adequate solution for micro-dust removal or for the prevention of the build-up of fly. Several well-known textile-machinery manufacturers have published patents, which offer different solutions to the dust and fly problem[280–283].

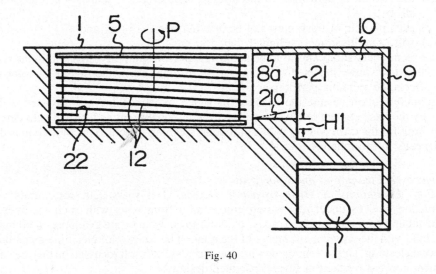

Fig. 40

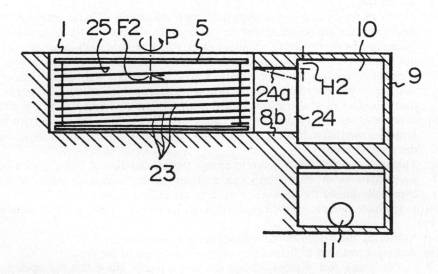

Fig. 41

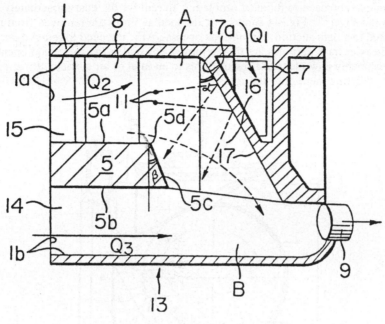

Fig. 42

A device patented by Parks-Cramer[282] uses a relatively low-velocity suction to remove trash continuously from each trash box of the rotor machine; it then intermittently produces a sudden surge in the suction to remove collected fly and dust. A similar approach by Zinser[284] involves the trash boxes being connected to a central suction point at which the suction rate is controlled by a shut-off valve. Periodic opening of the valve allows cleaning with a high degree of suction. Fig. 43 shows an interesting design patented by Schubert & Salzer[285]. It involves a tapered trash chamber with two additional openings (220) and (24). The first (220) is an added-air inlet; the second (24) is to facilitate the provision of a continuous low suction rate. By these means, fine dust and fly can be removed without interruption of the smooth flow of fibres to the rotor. The heavier dirt and other impurities are removed at the lower end of the trash chamber.

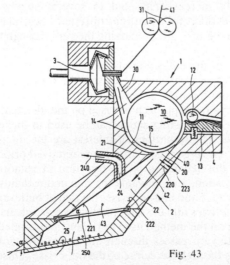

Fig. 43

A fairly unique approach to the dust problem is to remove the dust immediately fibres are separated from the sliver[286]. Fig. 44 shows that, as soon as fibres are removed from the sliver, they are subjected to a light suction, through the opening AF_1, intended to remove the light dust particles. The heavier trash particles are then removed as usual at (5). A second opening, AF_2, exposes the presumably now-cleaned flow of fibres to an inlet of air sufficient to straighten the fibres while accelerating them onto the rotor.

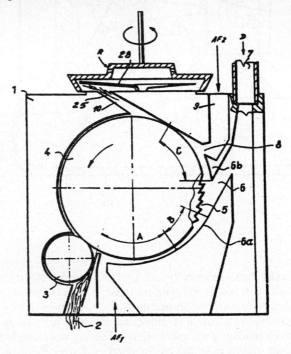

Fig. 44

5.1.7.3 *Self-cleaning Rotors*

The possible savings in production costs that would be effected if periodic cleaning of rotors could be avoided or if the period between successive cleanings could be substantially increased has led to several studies into the design of self-cleaning rotors. The work reported followed four different lines, namely:

    (i)   spinning with 'back take-off', i.e., removing the yarn through the centre of the rotor base;
    (ii) modifying the shape of the collecting groove;
    (iii) drilling holes of different sizes and angles into the rotor periphery; and
    (iv) optimizing the air-flow through the rotor.

5.1.7.4 *'Back Take-off'*

The first approach is based on the idea that, when twist is being inserted into the collected fibres, the twisting action can be used to make the fibres brush the impurities from the rotor groove. The impurities of interest are the micro-dust particles. The technique therefore assumes that the large trash particles are removed prior to fibre collection in the rotor groove. The basis of this technique is the direction of rotation of the yarn in the peripheral-twist zone. Inward rotation, i.e., towards the maximum radius of the rotor, pushes particles into the bottom of the groove and thus increases the rate of build-up of the dust deposits. Outward rotation tends to eject particles into the rotor base and keep a cleaner groove[287, 288]. The direction of rotation will depend on the method used to remove the formed yarn from the rotor, i.e., 'front take-off' – where the yarn passes through the centre of a doffing tube – or 'back take-off' – where the yarn passes through the centre of the rotor base. Observations have shown

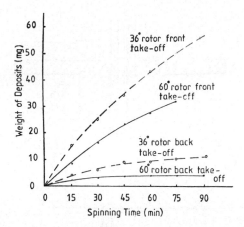

Fig. 45
The effects of the direction of yarn take-off for two shapes of rotor groove on the build-up of deposits

(see Fig. 45[287]) that the effect is independent of clockwise or anti-clockwise rotation of the rotor itself or of whether S or Z twist is inserted into the yarn. Other reports imply that 'back take-off' can present costly engineering-design and construction problems[289].

5.1.7.5 Modifications to the Collecting-groove Profile During the early development of rotor-spinning machines, considerable effort was directed into optimizing the design of the rotor profile in order to improve fibre transfer to the collection groove and more efficient twist insertion. The objective was to improve yarn strength. Studies showed, however, that modifying the rotor profile also affected the degree of rotor-fouling even when front take-off was employed[287–289].

What may be a suitable profile for improving yarn strength is not necessarily effective for self-cleaning; as a result, the outcome would be the characteristic fall-off in yarn strength with increasing build-up of deposits. The fact that a significant number of patents are still being published may be taken as evidence that development work is actively being pursued in this area[290, 291, 294, 295].

Figures 46, 47, and 48 show typical patented rotor profiles, all designed for the now widely used 'side-feed' fibre transfer to the rotor. In each design, there is a sliding wall (designated 4, 1*a*, and 12, respectively), down which the fibres slide towards the collection groove (5, 1*b*, and 11, respectively). As shown in the figures, there are several angles that characterize the profile of the collecting-groove region. The angle of the slide wall must not be too shallow or fibre transfer to the groove will be poor, yet not too steep or dust accumulation will increase. From the point of view of self-cleaning, it is the angles defining the groove itself that have the greatest effect, e.g., B, D, and E in Fig. 46. It is self-evident that the more obtuse the angle of the rotor groove, i.e., for larger angles E and D, the easier will be the removal of deposits by the rotating fibres. From a comparison of the three profiles, Fig. 46 would therefore be expected to have the best self-cleaning effect.

Nield and Abadeer[287, 288] reported that, when the total angle, B + E, is 60° (i.e., with a 60° rotor) a better cleaning effect was apparent even with front take-off. Fig. 45 shows results obtained for both a 36° rotor and a 60° rotor. The 36° rotor collected deposits more rapidly, although with front take-off it had a longer maximum spinning time. The tighter rotor groove was also observed to give better yarn strength. With regard to yarn properties obtainable from different profiles, it is the amount of rotor surface in contact with the yarn tail that is important. With the profile of Fig. 48, it is clear that, as the yarn tail rotates on its axis through the action of twist, the surface fibres, including wrapper fibres, on the yarn tail may become more tightly bound to the yarn because of the added frictional contact at the position (8). This, however, assumes that the

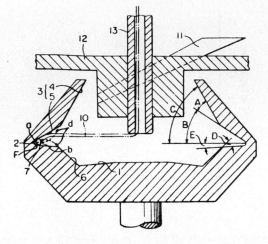

Fig. 46

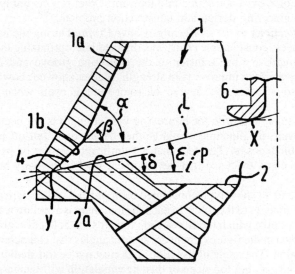

· Fig. 47

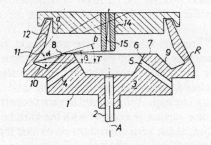

Fig. 48

opposing frictional forces at (8) accompanying the circumferential rotation of the yarn tail relative to the rotor are small. This rotor would therefore be more suited to improving yarn strength than to improving self-cleaning. Of the three profiles, Fig. 47 would appear the best compromise. The narrower angle than that shown in Fig. 46 facilitates greater compacting of the fibres and possible contact of the yarn, with the rotor bottom surface at 2*a* giving a good degree of additional binding of surface fibres, all of which add up to improvement in yarn strength.

Although not to the same degree as that shown in Fig. 46, this profile may be assumed to give a better cleaning action than that shown in Fig. 48. There are fewer rotor projections, such as (8) in Fig. 48, to hinder trash movement to the rotor base.

5.1.7.6 Drilled Holes in the Rotor The idea of drilling holes in the rotor periphery to remove possible accumulations of deposits is not novel. The holes are not intended to generate the air-flow needed for the transfer of fibres from the opening roller to the collecting groove, as is the case with BD200 rotors. Their size and positions are therefore different. Previous work with peripheral holes was mainly concerned with the spinning of wool fibres and involved large-diameter rotors. Although the holes allowed a degree of trash ejection, their suction effect interfered with the fibre arrangement and twist propagation in the rotor groove and made spinning possible only at uneconomically high twist factors. When short fibres were tried, the high twist factors and the high loss of fibres through the holes made the technique impracticable.

Recent patents show that the repositioning of the holes from the rotor groove to the outer radius of the rotor base is a more promising proposition[296–298]. Fig. 49 illustrates a self-cleaning-rotor design utilizing waste-removal holes. The holes (8) can vary in number (50 – 150) and size (0.5 – 3 mm) but must be positioned no closer than 4 mm from the rotor groove. It is interesting to note that the complexity of the rotor profiles described earlier would not appear to be necessary when this technique is applied. It is also claimed that dust accumulation is significantly less than with the other self-cleaning rotors[298]. The total waste removed is reported to be up to 1%, based on the weight of yarn spun. The inference is that fibre loss would be significant even though the lint removed had a low mean fibre length and a high short-fibre content. Yarn quality and spinning performance were claimed to have improved when the waste holes were drilled into the rotor, and the yarns produced gave less lint-shedding during knitting.

5.1.7.7 Optimizing Air-flow in the Rotor The air-flow patterns resulting from the two most widely used methods for producing a vacuum in the rotor (i.e., self-pumping rotors and external suction) show differences in their usefulness for rotor self-cleaning[299]. Louis[300] studied the effectiveness of the two systems by adding to a double-carded, second-drawn sliver 1250 mg of carefully graded trash particles, typical of cotton impurities. Table 5.1 gives details of the additions and of the average amount of impurities removed from the rotor by the air-flow from the two systems.

It is clear that the external suction gave the better cleaning effect. With the self-pumping system, the under-pressure is dependent on the spinning speed of the rotor, whereas with the external-suction system the under-pressure is independent of the rotor speed and can be kept at its optimum level irrespective of variations in rotor speed. The external-suction system, nevertheless, has a significant limitation in that the discharge of the air usually takes place over the rim of the rotor, i.e., through the gap between the rotor cover and the rotor rim. The air at this position is subjected to a strong friction drag and a rapid constriction of its flow path. As a result, dust and trash particles being carried in the air-flow as it is exhausted become deposited on the rotor rim and eventually end up within the rotor groove[301]. In an attempt to improve this method, several patented designs have been published, these being aimed at modifying the outlet over the rotor rim[301–305]. Fig. 50 illustrates one such design[303]. The exhaust for the air-flow (5) is machined in the casing (2), which fits into the rotor inlet. Being shielded by the flanged doffing tube (6), the yarn tail cannot be disturbed. However, the external suction, when connected to the exhaust channel, will cause the air entering the rotor from both the hole (4) in the doffing tube and the transport tube (30) to carry the entrained dust and trash particles away from the rotor wall (13). Because the constriction of the air-flow is more gradual, particle deposition is less likely to occur.

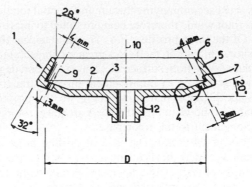

Fig. 49

Table 5.1
Comparison of Self-pumping Rotors and External Suction for Self-cleaning of Rotors

Lot	Trash Added to Sliver	Frame A (Self-pump)				Frame B (External Air)			
		Test 1	Test 2	Average	Ranking	Test 1	Test 2	Average	Ranking
A	Control (no additive)	9.7	15.2	12.45	2	5.0	0.3	2.65	1
B	50% Fine/50% coarse	30.3	27.9	29.10	5	148.6	136.7	142.65	5
C	10% Coarse-leaf particles	13.4	30.4	21.90	3	154.4	197.2	175.80	6
D	100% Dust	9.0	11.8	10.40	1	58.7	64.6	61.65	2
E	50% Dust/25% fine/25% coarse	36.4	14.5	25.45	4	112.8	114.5	113.65	3
F	100% Fine-leaf particles	44.1	24.5	34.30	6	117.1	130.7	123.90	4

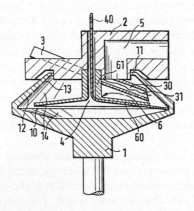

Fig. 50

5.2   The Production of Fine Rotor-spun Yarns
5.2.1   Introduction

There is no doubt to-day that technically rotor-spun yarns as fine as 10 tex can be produced[306–310]. However, for commercial success, the spinning must be done under realistic conditions; that is, the economics must be competitive with those of traditional processes. It is reported that open-end-spinning mills in Czechoslovakia have been successfully producing fine yarns – of 20 tex – since 1977[310]. The problem is that what is an economically sound programme for a mill in Czechoslovakia is not necessarily so for one in Lancashire. Hence, although considerable progress has been achieved for rotor technology in the area of fine yarn, it cannot be stated categorically that the economic count limit has indeed shifted from 25 tex (24 N_e) to a finer value. In addition, the progress achieved has had to involve some complementary modifications to established knitting, weaving, and finishing techniques, and thus the economics for fine rotor-spun yarns have become more complex. The economics of spinning fine rotor-spun yarns are now a function, not only of geography and political ideology, but also of the organization and management of the textile company concerned. The company whose final product is the spun yarn may find fine rotor-spun yarns non-profitable, whereas the vertically organized company may find it an answer to the continual competitive market demand for new products in the apparal sector.

In the spinning of fine rotor-spun yarns, three factors must be given careful consideration[310]:
> the choice of raw materials;
> the sliver preparation; and
> the choice of machine variables.

5.2.2 The Choice of Raw Material

The choice of raw material, and of cotton fibres in particular, is a very important factor, since the minimum number of fibres admissible in the yarn cross-section is much higher for rotor-spun yarns than for ring-spun yarns. This means that, in using the same fibre, rotor-spun yarns cannot be spun to as fine a count as ring-spun yarns. A first significant parameter of the raw material is therefore the fibre fineness. It can be said that the fibre fineness governs the spinning limit, efficiency, minimum twist, and yarn quality as well as the handle of the end-product. Consequently, finer fibres should be selected for rotor-spinning than for ring-spinning[311]; the increase in the number of fibres in the yarn cross-section can reduce strength loss due to the poor fibre parallelization[312].

The fibre strength is another major parameter influencing the quality of a rotor-spun yarn. As might be expected, a stronger fibre yields a stronger yarn.

Fibre length is the third important parameter governing the quality of rotor-spun yarn, and, because irregularity plays such a large part with finer yarns, every effort must be made to optimize the yarn evenness. In spinning finer yarns, the fibre length must be increased, and it has been found that the unevenness of open-end-spun yarns reaches a minimum with fibre lengths of approximately 40 mm[311]. A small percentage of long-fibre belts in fine rotor-spun yarn improves the strength of the yarn owing to the reinforcement of the yarn body through belts. It has been observed that these long belts extend during tensile straining of the yarn and thereby increase the lateral compression on the yarn core. Cyclic tensile tests at 60% of the average breaking extension show that the presence of long-fibre belts restricts core-fibre slipping during axial straining and reduces the extent of permanent deformation[313, 314].

In one study, statistical analysis of the data reported showed that the fibre length, fineness, tenacity, and maturity together accounted for 80% of the variation in count–strength product (CSP), fibre tenacity, inevitably, being the most influential property[315]. An expression for predicting CSP and yarn irregularity was derived as:

$$\mathrm{CSP} = k \left(\frac{lS}{f} \right)^{0.35} ,$$

where S is the fibre tenacity at 3-mm gauge length (gf/tex) as measured by the Stelometer, f is the Micronaire reading, and l is the 50% span length in mm as measured by the Digital Fibrograph. It was also found that:

$$U^2 = \left\{ 5.62 \left(\frac{f}{l} \right) h + 0.2050 \right\} d + U_s^2,$$

where U is the irregularity of the yarn, U_s is the irregularity of the sliver, h is the hank of the sliver, and d is the draft.

Other work has also shown that relatively small changes in Micronaire value can cause large differences in processing and yarn quality[316].

Prihoda and Berankova[317] report that, in the course of selecting cotton fibres, the values of the fibre fineness, length, ripeness, i.e., maturity, and strength should comply with the following requirements:

(a) average fibre fineness 1.7 dtex;
(b) effective fibre length 32 mm;
(c) fibre breaking length 26–28 km;
(d) percentage of ripe fibres in excess of 80%.

5.2.3   The Requirements of Sliver Preparation

Although it is possible to spin a 100-tex (5.9s N_e), as well as a 20-tex (29.5s N_e) yarn on the same rotor-spinning machine, certain criteria must be observed in sliver preparation for the production of fine yarns[318].

In principle, the rotor-spinning machine is capable of operating over a wide total-draft ratio. But the spinning of a fine yarn from thick sliver does not give an adequate spinning performance. Technically, what is of importance is the opening draft between the feed roller and the opening roller. The shorter the residence time of the fed fibre in this combing zone, the gentler is the opening process. It is therefore preferable to feed thin slivers at high speed, rather than thick slivers at low speed. Thus, finer yarns require finer slivers. For example, over a yarn-linear-density range of 33–100 tex, a sliver linear density of c. 4 ktex is recommended and, for 25–33 tex, a suitable sliver linear density is 3.4 ktex; for 20–25 tex, however, a sliver linear density within the range 2.5–3 ktex should be used[318].

Sliver variations, such as those detected by determining the mass of 1-m lengths, will lead to yarn-count variations and a reduction in the running performance. Although this is not peculiar to fine-yarn spinning, the effects are disproportionately greater. When a range is reached where c. 100 fibres are in the yarn cross-section, each fibre will amount to c. 1% of the yarn mass, so the sliver irregularity should not exceed a CV of 4%, particularly for fine slivers, and the coefficient of variation for the 1-m lengths tested should be less than 1.5%. These figures can be obtained by the use of two draft passages, with sliver-levelling taking place either at the card or at the first-draft passage[318].

A small soil particle of only 0.2 mg can exert a force of the order of 10 gf (98.1 mN) on the yarn end under the influence of centrifugal force. A coarse yarn may withstand this additional strain, but a fine yarn will not. Hence it is necessary to obtain a high degree of purity by the use of modern cleaning equipment and cards[318]. The impurity level should not exceed 3 mg/g of sliver.

The more parallel the fibre orientation in the drafted sliver, the better will be the fibre arrangement in the rotor groove and ultimately in the yarn. This means a minimum of two draft passages, possibly three, if combed sliver is used[318].

Particularly in the processing of fine blended yarns, the question of homogeneous blending and blending uniformity plays a large rôle. It should be stressed that inhomogeneity may be tolerated in coarse-yarn spinning but will cause problems of yarn quality in the spinning of finer yarns. For this reason, special attention should be paid to the careful mixing of the various components, the number of doublings in the drafting passages being the most significant[318]. Fine slivers are readily subject to draft faults such as the splitting of the web or licking up of fibres, which ruins the desired final assembly of the fibre mass. Hence the number of draft passages has to be limited to the point beyond which splitting could occur. For the same reason, the delivery speed of the drawframe must be reduced for very fine slivers. Speeds should not exceed 300 m/min for a sliver linear density of up to 3 ktex, and care should be taken in coiling the sliver into sliver cans[318].

5.2.4   The Choice of Rotor-machine Variables

It has been found that a reduction of the total spinning draft leads to a reduced end-breakage rate and an improvement in the uniformity and tenacity of the spun yarn. Over-all draft ratios between 160 and 170 give the best results. Similar studies conducted at the Institute for Textile Technology, Reutlingen, Germany, showed the breaking tenacity of the yarn to rise when the total draft was reduced from 285 to 95. The same effect was seen for the breaking elongation, and the hairiness of the yarn was distinctly reduced[318].

For opening-roller settings, there is a practical lower limit to the opening speed[318]. It has been observed that, as the speed of the opening roller increases, the incidence of fibre breakage also goes up. The increase in fibre breakage has been attributed to the increase in the value of the carrying factor, i.e., the number of wire points per fibre[319]. In other words, the fibres are acted upon a greater number of times when the speed of the opening roller is increased[319]. The optimum speed does not give the best value for all the yarn properties. A good regularity requires low opening-roller and rotor speeds, whereas high tenacity and elongation at break require high speeds to be used[320–323].

The effects of saw-tooth and pinned clothing have been studied by using the Platt Saco Lowell Rotospin 883. The results reported showed that there is no difference in the quality of the spun yarns when either type of clothing is used under identical spinning conditions. Other studies involving different makes of machine showed the pinned-type clothing to be a more effective opener. The criterion for choosing the best clothing to use will therefore rest mainly on the price and replacement cycle (or wear rate). On the basis of information provided by machine makers, the pinned type has the lowest wear rate[324].

Disturbing air forces are one of the main reasons for the difference between the fibre configuration and extent in rotor- and ring-spun yarns. In spinning fine yarns, such disturbance must therefore be kept to a minimum, particularly in the rotor unit, where the exit of the feed tube in the rotor cover extends into the rotor. The position of the feed-tube axis in relation to the rotor wall and the cross-section of the feed tube have proved to be critical. On the Rieter M1/1 machine, changes have been made to shorten the distance of free flight of the fibres from the opening roller into the rotor.

This redesign of the geometry of the fibre feed into the rotor is reported to have improved the fibre alignment and parallelization in the yarn and thereby narrowed the difference between ring- and rotor-spun yarn characteristics.

Texas Tech University Research Center is reported to have successfully spun yarn of 7.2 tex (82s N_e) on the modified M1/1 'U' unit at a rotor speed of 55 000 r/min with a twist factor of 2.98. The yarn had only 49 fibres in the cross-section[325].

The choice of rotor diameter must be made with regard to the raw material, staple length, yarn count, and rotor speed[326]. The recommendations in Table 5.2 have been made[326].

Table 5.2

Rotor Diameter (mm)	Staple Length (mm)	Rotor Speed (r/min)	Linear Density (tex)	N_e
40	< 32	> 45 000	25–16	(24–37)
48	< 40	30–70 (× 10³)	100–20	(5.9–30)
56	< 50	30–60 (× 10³)	166–25	(3.6–24)

For spinning fine cotton yarns at high speeds, a small diameter is recommended[327, 328]. The small-diameter rotor gives a lower centripetal force, even at extremely high speeds[327], which would result in lower yarn tensions. However, rotors with smaller diameters may require higher twist coefficients than those with larger diameters if the running properties of the yarn are to be kept the same. Studies have shown that, at a speed of 70 000 r/min and above, the minimum twist value rises when a 48-mm-diameter rather than a 56-mm-diameter rotor is used[326]. A rise also occurs with 40-mm-diameter rotors but only at much higher speeds. A 40-mm-diameter rotor is recommended for cotton yarns, but in processing some man-made fibres, where comparatively high twist factors are required, larger rotor diameters should be chosen[326]. The width of the rotor groove has a pronounced effect on the strength of fine yarns. Narrow-grooved rotors are recommended for consistently producing strong yarns[328]. Wide-grooved rotors will give hairier yarns and in many cases produce more imperfections as measured by the Uster Imperfection Indicator. It should be noted, however, that the narrow-grooved rotor will probably become loaded with residue more easily than the wide-grooved rotor[329]. The effect of the rotor speed on yarn properties depends on the make and type of the rotor-spinning machine as well as on the rotor design[330]. High rotor speeds demand high twist coefficients to prevent the running performance and yarn quality from deteriorating significantly[326]. Any factor that increases the twisting torque at the yarn-formation point (for example, high rotor speeds, large-diameter rotors, and grooves in the yarn-take-off navel) produce yarns with poor fibre orientation and a high short-term variability[326]. Measurements of the fibre orientation in the rotor groove have indicated that the fibre parallelization became worse at high rotor speeds. This and the findings of the effect of the twisting torque indicate that obtaining a good-quality, relatively fine open-end-spun yarn at high rotor speeds can be difficult. It requires a thorough knowledge of the factors that affect open-end-spun-yarn quality at high speeds and involves a compromise between rotor diameter, rotor groove, fibre type, etc., to meet a particular requirement[330].

The grooved doffing tube permits yarns to be spun at lower twist factors, but often at the expense of the yarn strength, extension, and visual rating. Modifications involving various surface coatings and inserts to obtain the low twist but better yarn properties have been included on several makes of machine[331–340]. However, it would appear that, to improve the production and quality of fine yarns, particularly at high rotor speed, further development work is still required in this area of the rotor-spinning unit.

5.3   Rotor-spinning of Man-made Fibres and Blends
5.3.1   Advantages and Disadvantages

Since the introduction of rotor-spinning, the production of blended natural and man-made-fibre rotor-spun yarns, particularly cotton–polyester-fibre blends, has held a special interest[341–345]. One important requirement in the manufacture of blended-fibre yarns is the degree of homogeneity in blending their components throughout the lengths of yarns spun and the uniform distribution of the individual fibre components in the yarn cross-section. In ring-spinning, a certain deblending occurs after the drawframe, since the longer fibres, usually polyester fibres, have a tendency to move to the yarn core, while the shorter ones tend to be bound into the surface of the yarn. For rotor-spinning, the doubling effect that occurs in the rotor after the complete separation down to individual fibres is well known to result in a homogeneous fibre distribution in the yarn cross-section. It is this feature that has raised the interest in blended rotor-spun yarns; it provides an opportunity, by correct use of the rotor-spinning process, to produce polyester-fibre–cotton blended-fibre yarns not only more economically but also with improved yarn quality[343, 344]. However, some of the properties of man-made fibres can impose limitations on the use of the rotor-spinning process[341, 342].

In the first place, the dielectric properties of the fibres themselves may cause a build-up of static charges on the fibres during processing. In the second place, the surface of the fibres, especially that of dull or matt fibres, may become an aggressive agent, damaging the machine parts that are liable to come into contact with the fibres during spinning. In addition, it is not only a low fibre strength but also fibre brittleness that is partly responsible for fibre damage, shortening, and the consequent rotor-dust accumulation[341, 342]. In choosing man-made fibres for rotor-spinning, particularly polyester fibre, either in blends or in 100% form, the properties discussed below should be given careful attention[346, 347].

5.3.2   Staple Length

In the processing of polyester fibres, the use of staple lengths of either 30 or 32 mm has proved a definite advantage, especially for finer yarns[343, 346, 347]. The anchoring of the fibre in the sliver is principally achieved by fibre–fibre friction, and thus the force required to remove a fibre from the sliver will increase with its staple length. Measurements of the driving moment of the opening roller operating on different staple lengths verify this relationship[343].

In ring-spinning, 38–40-mm staples have proved to be easily processed and are predominantly used[343]. But, in rotor-spinning, as the sliver is presented to the opening roller, the longer staple length has a higher resistance to extraction, leading to abrasion and deposits, which include oligomers from the fibre surface. This fibre debris contains a large number of short fibres, which often create yarn defects. Reported results have shown that an excessive amount of fibre damage occurs when 38–40-mm staples are used[346].

The shorter staple length can call for smaller rotors. Thus the energy consumption required for driving the rotors can be reduced. Spinning 40-mm staple fibres on a 40-mm-diameter rotor would lead to a distinct increase in the number of wrappers. Moreover, the spinning twist would have to be increased considerably in order to provide the necessary twisting moment in the rotor groove[343].

In ring-spinning, the longer staple length has the advantage of reducing the hairiness of the yarn. But, since rotor-spun yarns inherently have less hairiness than ring-spun yarns, there can be no objection to reducing the staple length from this aspect. Furthermore, equally strong rotor-spun yarns can be produced from a 32-mm fibre as from a 40-mm fibre[343], with the advantage of obtaining optimum yarn uniformity[347].

5.3.3 Fibre Fineness

It has been reported that the optimum linear density/filament for rotor-spinning is 1.5 den (1.67 dtex)[346]. Increasing this value can reduce rotor deposits but will produce poorer yarn properties. Conversely, reducing the value below 1.5 den increases deposits while improving yarn evenness and strength.

The advantage of finer fibres is that, while maintaining a minimum number of fibres in the cross-section, one can raise the fine-yarn count limit for rotor-spun yarns considerably. Further advantages are the ability to reduce yarn twist and increase breaking tenacity. But the finer the fibre, the greater is the risk of fibre damage. Firstly, because the absolute strength of the individual fibres will be less; and, secondly, the anchoring force on the fibre in the sliver will be greater, a larger force being required to remove the individual fibres[343].

The limitations in using extremely fine fibres will probably come not from the actual rotor-spinning process but from the preparatory processes, particularly carding. For fine rotor-spun yarns, a well-prepared sliver is a major factor in obtaining good yarn properties and spinning performance. It remains to be seen whether it will be possible to produce acceptable slivers from such extremely fine fibres economically, so that the possible technological advantages will not be outweighed by the higher fibre price[343].

5.3.4 Fibre Crimp

Synthetic fibres are mechanically crimped to facilitate their processing during the different stages of spinning. The crimp introduced is not always very durable and in conventional spinning is gradually lost in the ensuing processing stages prior to spinning. In rotor-spinning, the number of processing stages is considerably reduced, and thus greater consideration has to be given to crimp level and crimp permanence.

In the selection of polyester fibres, it should be remembered that low-crimp fibres have better processing properties, i.e., they can more easily be twisted into yarn and produce stronger yarns[343].

Highly crimped fibres perform poorly in open-end spinning for the following reasons[346]:
- (a) they have greater resistance to extraction from the sliver by the opening roller, and this resistance can lead to fibre damage and rotor deposits; and
- (b) they produce an uneven yarn because they do not flow smoothly in the duct between the opening roller and the rotor; furthermore they do not lie in a compact mass in the 'V' of the rotor groove.

Fibres with low crimp levels give higher yarn strength, fewer yarn defects, and a reduced number of ends down. Fibres with too low a crimp level or permanence will, however, have a poor card-web cohesion and result in a poorly drawn sliver. Care therefore has to be taken in order to obtain the optimum crimp balance between sliver preparation and spinning, that is, the fibre crimp should last through carding, but the drawing process should remove most of it[346].

5.3.5 Tenacity

High-tenacity polyester fibres are reported to perform better than lower-strength versions because they minimize the strength loss of open-end-spun yarns, suffer less breakage, and therefore produce fewer rotor deposits[346].

On the whole, it is claimed that 1.5-den/fil (1.67-dtex/fil), 32-mm high-tenacity polyester fibres with round cross-section give the best spinning performance for 100% polyester fibre and blends, as well as the strongest open-end-spun yarns[346]. This does not, however, reflect the fact that different end-uses will necessitate the use of different polyester-fibre types. For knitwear, low-pill polyester fibre is commonly used, and the problems experienced with the low-pill material are more acute than those with standard polyester fibre, especially in the degree of rotor deposits. However, it has been observed that a low-level blend with cotton of up to 35% polyester fibre readily reduces processing difficulties. This applies not only to rotor deposits but also to static problems[348, 349].

The choice of fibre material is always accompanied by the question of special surface finishes. As is well known, man-made fibres can experience a build-up of static charges on the fibre surface during processing; hence the necessity arises to use an effective anti-static agent, as well as a lubricant, as a surface finish. Better performance comes from polyester fibre with a lubricant level slightly lower than that normally required for ring-spinning. More opening-roller wrap-ups are encountered when the fibre contains a high lubricant level. However, too low a lubricant level causes static problems at carding and a high rotor deposit at spinning[346]. In cases where electrostatic charges are a problem, the further addition of 0.05–0.1% of an effective anti-static agent is recommended[348]. Eastman Laboratories[346] have evaluated several commercial lubricants with the object of determining which lubricant reduces fibre-to-metal friction most significantly and which gives less rotor deposits and abrasion. Certain lubricants recommended for ring-spinning were found to be suitable for open-end spinning.

Of equal, if not greater importance is the need to ensure that the correct atmospheric conditions exist during spinning. The ambient temperature should not be lower than 23°C, and the relative humidity should be between 50 and 55%[348].

When inorganic pigments, usually TiO_2, are included in synthetic fibres as delustring agents, they usually cause severe wear on various parts of the rotor-spinning units, particularly the opening rollers and the rotors[350].

The content of titanium oxide in matt fibres is usually up to 0.5%. So-called half-matt, or semi-dull, fibres containing considerably less TiO_2 therefore provide a better solution. A further reduction in the wear rate can evidently be obtained through blending[348]. Schmidt and Dorsch[350] report a process for the production of high-matt non-pigmented acrylic fibres; a high-matt effect is provided by light-scattering voids present in the fibres. These fibres allow the 100% matt rotor-spun yarns to be spun without incurring wear problems.

Experienced spinners are well acquainted with the fact that not only do fibres of the same generic type from different suppliers differ in their processing behaviour, but fibres of different batches from the same producers can also give drastic variation in both spinning performance and resultant yarn properties. Quality control of the input fibre is therefore necessary to ensure a constant efficiency throughout the spinning programme. It would appear that most problems are caused through an uneven application of finish to the fibre surface, and Vasatko et al.[351] have therefore developed a procedure whereby measuring the specific resistance, the electrostatic charge, and the number of passages through a Spinn–Taxer device[351] before wrapping occurs makes it possible to predict the spinning performance of most fibres.

When materials show a very low specific resistance and survive a large number of passages on the Spinn–Taxer, a good spinning performance may be expected even for fine yarns and at relative humidities that are lower than standard. Materials with a specific resistance of 1500 MΩ and a four-passage limit on the Spinn–Taxer will cause difficulties, particularly at low relative humidities and with fine yarns. Materials with a specific resistance over 1500–2000 MΩ and fewer than four passages on the Spinn–Taxer are generally unsuitable for spinning.

5.3.6 Sliver Preparation

When sliver blends are prepared for rotor-spinning, the uniformity of the blend requires special attention. The redoubling of the fibres in the rotor will produce a good fibre distribution in the yarn cross-section, but it is incapable of compensating for long-term irregularities. There are principally two methods of component blending: flock-blending and draft-sliver-blending; which of these two is chosen depends, for a polyester-fibre–cotton blend, on whether the cotton component used is carded or combed[348].

It has been shown that the use of combed cotton instead of carded cotton does not improve the yarn tenacity. The values of the other yarn properties also lie within the accepted normal region of scatter. Hence it is practicable to replace the combed-cotton component with a carded-cotton one[348].

For a carded-cotton component in the blend, both blending systems are feasible. However, with draft-sliver-blending, even after the second passage of drawing, the sliver is still basically in a stripe form composed of 36 partial slivers, half of them cotton and the other half polyester-fibre. If sliver-blending is used, autolevelling should therefore be carried out at the card with two or three drawframe passages prior to spinning[348]. The stretch–break–rebreak approach before drawframe blending is still argued for, but it is not yet widely used in the spinning of short-staple blends[352].

5.3.7 Rotor-spinning Parameters

The optimum twist factors for man-made-fibre rotor-spun yarns are low compared with those for cotton yarns of the equivalent counts[353, 354]. With acrylic fibres, the maximum yarn strength occurs for values of twist close to 120 (turns/m) tex$^{1/2}$; for polyester-fibre yarns, the optimum value is about 140, and for viscose yarns it is below 120. The highest elongation, however, always occurs at twist multipliers below 120, whatever the fibre. It was also found that the deteriorating influence of increased total draft on the yarn regularity only became evident at high twist levels[354].

Work has shown that, for yarns of a high linear density, the type of opening roller does not affect yarn characters in any important manner, but, in the medium-to-fine range, better results are found with an opening roller that ensures a smooth separation of the fibres. A type OK–36 opening roller, in which the teeth of clothing are inclined at an angle of 90°, the tooth height is 1.2 mm, and the separation between the teeth is 4 mm, giving a density of 14 teeth per cm^2, is adequate for viscose and acrylic fibre, and type OK–37, in which the angle is 99°, the tooth height is 2 mm, and the separation between the teeth is 4.7 mm, giving a density of 13.3 teeth per cm^2, gives good separation for polyester fibre[355].

The main problem in spinning man-made fibres and their blends is to separate the fibres without damaging them. Most man-made fibres are best processed at opening-roller speeds between 6000 and 7000 r/min[356–358].

The choice of a suitable rotor type and speed is usually made according to the yarn count and the proposed application of the resultant yarn. However, the yarn tension during rotor-spinning must not exceed a specific level, since the yarn quality will be impaired by mechanical stressing of the fibres on the surface of the yarn. The measured yarn tension is the product of the frictional force of the yarn at the doffing tube and the centrifugal force that acts on the yarn end in the rotor. Since coarse yarns can accommodate higher tensions than finer yarns, it is recommended that the yarn tension should be related to the linear density of the yarn. The linear-density-related centrifugal force, F_z/tex, which occurs during spinning, can be calculated from the relation [359]:

$$\frac{F_z}{\text{tex}} = \frac{1}{20\ 000} \times \frac{\pi R n}{30} \text{ cN/tex},$$

the rotor speed, n, and the diameter, R, being known. On the assumption that the spinning tension must not exceed 60% of the yarn strength, to avoid the problems of tension fluctuations, results have shown that there is an optimum value for F_z/tex.

In practical terms, this means that only small-diameter rotors should be used at high speeds. However, it must be noted that the rotor diameter/fibre length ratio should not be less than 1.0 and that small rotor diameters require higher yarn twist[359]. For a 38–40-mm staple length, a 48–56-mm rotor diameter will give the best compromise between yarn quality and productivity. For smaller rotors, the staple length should be 30–32 mm[357].

Higher rotor speeds lead to a steep rise in yarn tension, and the resulting yarn friction against the doffing tube may cause localized melting of synthetic fibres. Microscopical studies have shown that melt-points can occur at speeds of 45 000 r/min and upwards when a 56-mm rotor is used[357]. Polyester fibres were found to be more prone to localized melting.

In considering the effects of rotor speed, the effects of the doffing tube should also be considered[360]. In general, in spinning man-made fibres, smooth doffing tubes are recommended in preference to the notched type in order to keep the stresses on the yarn within acceptable limits[357].

It is clear from the above information that there are several interacting factors from which the optimum spinning conditions have to be determined. Barella and his co-workers[361, 362] have illustrated the advantages of using a mini-computer for rapid calculations in spinning trials involving several factors to establish the best conditions for a given fibre stock.

5.3.8 Comparison between Rotor-spun Yarns and Ring-spun Yarns Containing Polyester Fibre

Rotor-spun yarns containing polyester fibre are 20–30% weaker than ring-spun yarns of similar counts. But this strength disadvantage is reduced when plied rotor-spun yarns are compared with plied ring-spun yarns. It is believed that plying locks the wrapper fibres and forces them to contribute towards yarn strength[363]. Although blended rotor-spun yarns are weaker than their ring-spun counterparts, the addition of at least 50% polyester fibre in a polyester-fibre–cotton blend increases the yarn strength above that of the 100% cotton yarn and can improve the end-use performance of certain products[364, 365]. This is reportedly the case for terry cloths made with a 65–35 polyester-fibre–cotton rotor-spun yarn for the ground fabric and 100% cotton rotor-spun yarn for the pile[366].

Rotor-spun yarns containing polyester fibre, in addition to having a lower strength, also have a lower elongation at break[363, 367–369], but a more uniform appearance, less liveliness, less hairiness, and a higher bulk. Hot-air shrinkage is lower, but a higher shrinkage will occur in boiling water.

Cross-sectional fibre distribution differs between the two types of yarn. The spinning tension in ring-spinning causes cotton fibres to migrate to the outer yarn surface. For example, a 50–50 polyester-fibre–cotton ring-spun yarn will have 60% or more cotton in its surface-fibre content. The same count of yarn spun on a rotor-spinning machine will have a more even fibre blend on the yarn surface. This difference between the two yarns is readily seen in the appearance of the resultant fabrics. The fabric made from open-end-spun yarns will have a lighter shade and will exhibit a frosty appearance[363].

5.4 The Rotor-spinning of Wool
5.4.1 Overcoming the Problems

From the onset of commercial rotor-spinning, a disproportionately lower effort was directed towards development work in the long-staple sector, although several machine manufacturers had marketed various designs of long-staple rotor-spinning systems. The main factors that muted the interest in long-staple spinning were severe difficulties encountered in the spinning of wool fibres and the lack of success in the application of rotor-spun yarns in cut-pile carpets. To-day, this situation has changed. Possibly because the expected rapid growth in the short-staple sector did not materialize, as efforts to push rotor-spinning into finer and finer counts met with only limited success, several machine manufacturers have turned more attention to the longer- (if not exactly long-) staple sector. Wool fibres as well as man-made fibres, particularly acrylic fibres, can now be prepared in suitable top form for rotor-spinning. Yarns produced by such means are finding their way into new fabrics, especially for the knitting market.

The problems that did arise from spinning wool were associated with the characteristics of the wool fibre and the limited possible end-uses of such rotor-spun yarns, i.e., the longer staple length of wool, its general coarseness as a fibre, the presence of the wool scales, burrs, and remnant trash content, its crimp frequency, the greater sensitivity of wool with respect to specific mechanical stresses, and the major structural differences between rotor-spun yarn and classical ring-spun yarn[370].

In ring-spinning, the use of long-staple fibres can offer technical and economic advantages as far as both the yarn and the finished goods are concerned. But, in rotor-spinning, the fact that a larger rotor diameter must be used, as well as much lower rotor speeds and comparatively high twist factors, means that, whatever the advantages of the system, it must be considered carefully. The longer the fibres, the greater are the fibre breakage, rotor deposits, and fly[371]; long fibres are also prone to wrap about the yarn, to form the unwanted wrappers.

As important as the breaking of fibres is the possibility of rubbing off the wool scales. This usually occurs at the opening roller; the scales are then deposited into the rotor groove as a ring of dust and thus disrupt the spinning process[370]. The natural crimp of wool fibres produces a high fibre friction in the sliver feed, which can result in high fibre breakage and scale deposits.

5.4.2 Preparation of Fibre Stock

With respect to the properties of the fibres, the chosen staple length should be less than the inside rotor diameter. It is important that very long fibres are not present, since these can cause yarn breaks. The limit to the fibre coarseness depends largely on the machine type and even the machine model[372]. However, as a general rule of thumb, spinning is limited to a minimum of 90–120 fibres in the yarn cross-section.

It is advantageous in rotor-spinning to select wools with a low crimp frequency. However, decrimping of wool fibres can be achieved by back-washing in a solution of sodium bisulphite and drying under tension. This improves the spinning properties of the fibres but can also weaken the yarn. It is, however, recommended that merino-wool slivers should be back-washed prior to rotor-spinning[373]. The natural wool grease has the positive effect of producing low friction between the fibre and the surfaces of the spinning elements, but excessive fat content can lead to contamination of the opening rollers and rotors. A residual fat content of 0.5–0.7% should therefore not be exceeded, and this is normally the case with carbonized wools. With standard wool tops or scoured wools, the fat content is usually 1%, and longer scouring times may thus be required.

The purity of the spinning stock is of importance. Ideally, the wool sliver must be free of any vegetable matter, clumps, and dust particles. As well as high end-breaks due to build-up in the rotor groove, if the dust particles are abrasive, the opening-roller clothing as well as the rotor may wear excessively[372].

The tendency for wool fibres to break during separation is partly due to their lower fibre strength when compared with cotton or man-made fibres. Fine wools of effective length 40–50 mm are therefore recommended if 100% wool[374] or a blend of wool and man-made fibre[375] is to be spun.

The finer fibres offer the advantages of:

       a wider range of yarn counts;

       better yarn strength and processing properties; and

       an improvement in the harshness of handle in fabrics, this harshness being due to the different yarn structure.

A 70–30 blended-fibre yarn of Dralon acrylic fibre and lamb's wool, marketed under the name 'Scott et Laine', is reported to have performed well in knitting as well as giving competitive fabric properties[376]. As with short-staple rotor-spinning, back-doubling in the rotor gave the blended yarn a good homogeneity and a high evenness, which improved the appearance of the knitted fabrics, even of single-knitted fabrics, and a higher strength uniformity and elasticity than are obtained with conventional spun yarns.

Blends of cotton and wool, 75–25 wool–cotton, are also reported to have been processed satisfactorily at normal cotton twist factors for rotor-spinning[374]. Whether, in the case of blends of wool and man-made fibres, blending is done before or after combing, it is important that the sliver has a uniform composition after preparation. The preparatory drawing passages after combing can be on either cotton-type drawframes or needle-roller drawframes, like SACM's HE drawframe. For cotton drawframes, the linear density of the single sliver must be low, e.g., 6 ktex, since otherwise the fibres do not receive sufficient control[372]. In feeding wool slivers to the open-end-spinning machine, it was found that fine slivers with higher feeding speeds were opened more gently than coarse slivers with low feeding speeds. Sliver masses/unit length of between 3.5 and 4.5 g/m (i.e., ktex) are therefore recommended[377].

Stretch-breaking is an alternative method for preparing the spinning stock. Normal tops may be used for rotor-spinning if the staple length is reduced by stretch-breaking. The staple diagram can then be altered by breaking the longest fibres in several draft zones. Results have shown that, all other things being equal, broken slivers can be spun with about 20% less twist than for carded slivers[372].

5.4.3 *Improvements in the Rotor-spinning Machine*

For the relatively long wool fibre, the distance between the feed roller and the opening roller is critical. If the distance is too short, the wool fibre will be broken. On the RU–80, the distance between the feed roller and the opening roller has been increased by 40 mm, which enables fibres up to 3 in. (75 mm) long to be processed[377].

The diameter of the opening roller has also been increased in order to process fibres of up to 3 in. (75 mm). Moreover, the opening roller has been widened to enable bulky slivers to be handled[377]. Pinned-type opening rollers were found to give the best separation, independently of the type of lubricant used. When the yarn properties were considered, the results showed that pinned opening rollers with speeds of less than 7000 r/min gave the best properties[377]. An alternative opening process utilizes a fibre selector in conjunction with a double-apron-draft feed[372, 378]. The selector consists of a cylinder created by staggered lamellae, each of which takes the form of an equilateral triangle with rounded corners. The cylinder presses against a rubber-covered roller and acts as a draft cylinder, applying very high draft ratios. The fibre end is briefly nipped between the selector and the rubber-covered roller and is removed from the sliver without a hooked configuration. It is claimed that this system handles the fibres more gently than any opening-roller arrangement and is therefore a solution to the problems arising from the sensitivity of wool to the mechanical strain of the opening roller.

For long-staple rotor-spinning, rotor diameters of 90–100 mm are reported to give good spinning performance, particularly in spinning coarse yarns[377] 'Wrapper fibres' are characteristic of rotor-spun yarns and cannot be avoided completely, but they can be reduced in number by choosing an optimum relation between rotor size and fibre length. For the spinning of wool, rotors with V-grooves are preferred[377, 379], and rotors without additional surface coatings were found to give the best results[377]. Owing to the greater sensitivity of wool fibres to mechanical stresses during spinning, a smooth doffing tube is recommended, and certain lubricants were also found to be advantageous[379].

5.5 Speciality Yarns
5.5.1 *Possible Developments*

In an effort to expand further the areas of applications for rotor-spinning, a number of studies have been conducted into the production of speciality yarns, such as slub yarns, multicomponent yarns, and core-spun yarns. It was recognized that core-spun yarns could easily be produced commercially, but the study of novelty-yarn spinning is still in its infancy. However, with suitable modifications to the design of the rotor unit, a successful commercial system could be marketed.

5.5.2   Fancy Slub Yarns

Fancy slub yarns can be produced on rotor-spinning machines by varying the draft briefly in the sliver-feed and opening-roller system to give deliberately thick places in the yarn. In an alternative method, patented by Pittman[380], slubs or thick and thin places are produced through twist variations by changing the delivery speed of the yarn as it leaves the rotor. The method produces a unique slub yarn, which has a portion of high twist adjacent to the slub in the yarn, which has lower yarn twist.

A second technique based on twist variations is shown in Fig. 51[381]. The design of the system is such that the roving (12) is spun by a rotor housed in (14). The yarn leaves through a doffing tube (18) and passes through rollers (21, 23) to be wound onto the bobbin (28). A lever (20) with a roller at its end (19) swings randomly up and down to lengthen and shorten the yarn between the doff tube (18) and rollers (21, 23), which thereby speeds up and slows down the yarn leaving the doff tube.

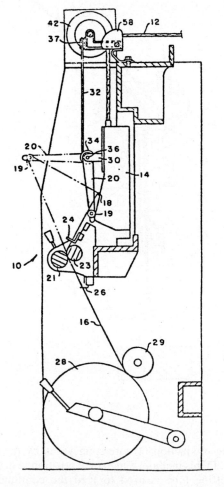

Fig. 51

5.5.3   Multicomponent Yarns

Multicomponent yarns consisting of two or more different yarns have been produced on modified rotor units, the aim being to spin a final yarn possessing all the desirable properties of the individual component yarns. Several problems have prevented the different techniques studied from progressing to at least the prototype stage. The major and the most common difficulty is the high yarn-breakage rate that occurs in the rotor. The frequency of yarn breaks is unacceptably high even when continuous-filament yarn is used as one component. Not only is the yarn-breakage rate a problem, but the resultant yarn quality is also usually poor, since it is extremely difficult to achieve proper tension control of the component yarns during spinning[382].

Fig. 52 shows a patented design that is reported to produce acceptable yarn quality[382]. With this rotor-spinning system, the multicomponent spun yarn has a construction in which the staple-fibre component is positioned at the centre and a continuous-filament yarn is wrapped around it. The resulting yarn is claimed to possess the desirable properties of both spun yarn and continuous-filament yarn. It is reported to have a good handle, similar to that of spun staple-fibre yarns, and also an excellent resistance to abrasion as a result of the continuous-filament wrapper. The yarn is claimed to be suitable for use in fabrics intended to be made into outer garments.

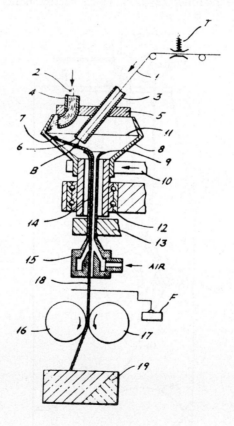

Fig. 52

5.5.4   Core-spun Yarns

A simple method for the production of core-spun yarns by the rotor-spinning system is described by Nield and Ali[383]. In this method, a feed tube positioned in the base of the rotor but in line with the axis of the doffing tube is used to feed the continuous-filamental core. The filamental-core component must be fed with a suitable tension, in the absence of which it will fly to the collecting surface of the rotor instead of remaining taut along the axis of the rotor. To start spinning, the staple-fibre yarn is pieced-up in the usual manner. The doffing tube is then made to rotate in the direction opposite to that of the rotor, and the continuous-filament core is next passed through the feed tube into the rotor. It attaches itself to the staple-fibre yarn being spun and is then pulled through the doffing tube by the staple-fibre yarn. The rotating doffing tube acts as a false-twister and pushes extra twist along the spun yarn to the peel-off point, while the rotation of the rotor wraps the spun yarn around the continuous-filament core[384]. Any type of material, including metallic wires of high torsional rigidities, can be used as cores to produce a core-spun yarn. Thus the technique could be used for producing high-insulation-covered electrical flex.

The possible advantages listed for producing core-spun yarns on a rotor-spinning system are[384]:

(a) the core-spun yarn is more likely to retain all the strength contributed by the core-component and the full length of the core-component, since the continuous filaments are not twisted during spinning and will therefore not suffer twist contraction;

(b) since the evenness of rotor-spun yarns is better than that of equivalent ring-spun structures, the evenness of rotor-core-spun yarns is expectedly better than that of equivalent ring-core-spun yarns;

(c) the bulkiness of rotor-core-spun yarns should be greater than that of the equivalent ring-spun structures, since the staple-fibre yarns spun on the rotor-spinning machine are more bulky than the equivalent yarns spun on the conventional system; thus a reduction in cloth set will be required to obtain the same cover from rotor-core-spun yarns;

(d) the production rate of the rotor-spinning machine, in terms of the yarn-delivery rate, is higher than that of the ring-spinning machine; hence the production rates for rotor-core-spun yarns should also be greater than those for conventional systems; and

(e) the direct winding of the core-spun yarn from the rotor onto cheeses or cones eliminates the rewinding process necessary for the conventional system and thus results in a significant cost reduction.

5.6 Post-spin-processing
5.6.1 General Considerations

When a new spinning process is implemented, the downstream processes are nearly always affected. Accordingly, the implications of rotor-spinning have had to be examined not only by the spinners but also by weavers, knitters, and finishers, because the yarn spun by the new process differs in its structure and properties from the familiar ring-spun yarn.

Studies have shown that, for a range of fabric types, rotor-spun yarns woven on Sulzer machines give effectively as good a performance as ring-spun yarns[385]. Table 5.3 shows the results of comparative ends-down tests. The woven cloths from rotor-spun yarns were easily distinguished by their more regular appearance and better cover compared with the ring-spun-yarn fabrics. The rotor-spun-yarn fabrics were found to take up about 10% more finishing liquor, which resulted in sharper prints and colours that were somewhat fuller. Table 5.4 shows the results of tests for fabric handle, cover, uniformity, and tensile strength on fabrics woven from rotor-spun and ring-spun yarns.

Investigations into the use of rotor-spun yarns on air-jet looms have resulted in the following conclusions[386–389]:

(a) there is a 40% reduction in the warp-breakage rate per 10 000 picks, with the weft-breakage rate remaining at a similar level to that for ring-spun yarns;

(b) there is an improved quality in the grey- and finished-fabric appearance; and

(c) machine speeds above 300 r/min, with weft-insertion rates from 900 to 1000 m/min, can be attained with rotor-spun yarns, without the need for accepting too high a stoppage rate[388].

Table 5.3
Results of Comparative Ends-down Tests

	Bed Sheets			Terry Fabric		Corduroy		Linings	
	Ring-spun, Electronically Cleaned	Open-end-spun Yarn Electronically Cleaned	Open-end-spun Yarn (Uncleaned)	Pile Warp Ring-spun	Pile Warp Yarn Open-end-spun	Ring-spun Yarn Weft Only	Open-end-spun Yarn	Ring-spun	Open-end-spun Yarn
Adjustment warp/weft	25.5/21.5	25.5/21.5	25.5/21.5	24.4/18.1	24.4/18.1	27/50	27/50	20/17.7	20/17.7
Count N_e warp/weft	16/16	16/16	16/16	24/2/16/1	24/2/16/1	20/14	20/14	20/20	20/20
Ends down per 100 000 picks				only N_e 16/1 tested	only N_e 16/1 tested				
Warp	5.61	6.9	2.89	14.15	6.94	3.86	3.60	1.4	6.5
Weft	0.69	2.1	4.39		3.05	1.38	1.30	0.6	0.3
Package-change stoppages	0.23	0.9	12.84		0.28			0.15	0.13
Total stoppages	6.53	9.85	20.12	14.15	10.27	5.24	4.90	2.15	6.93

Table 5.4
Handle, Cover, Uniformity, and Tensile Strength

		Ring-spun Yarn	Open-end-spun Yarn
1	Handle	Softer	Harder
2	Cloth cover	Less marked	More marked
3	Uniformity with high weft density	Less marked	More marked
4	Yarn tensile strength	Higher	Lower (10–30%)
5	Grab tensile test		
	grey goods	Higher	Lower
	warp	52	44 (about 15%)
6	Grab tensile test		
	grey goods	Higher	Lower
	weft	38	31.5 (about 17%)
7	Tensile strength, pretreated		
	warp without/with ML	Higher	Lower
		48/49	40.5/39.0
	weft without/with ML	Higher	Lower
		39/39	28.5/29.0
8	Tensile strength, wetted pieces	Higher	Lower
	warp without ML, mercerized	27	23.5
9	Tensile strength, wetted pieces	Higher	Lower
	weft without ML, mercerized	21.0	16.5
10	Tensile strength, wetted pieces	Higher	Lower
	warp with ML, mercerized	27.0	23.0
11	Tensile strength, wetted pieces	Higher	Lower
	weft with ML, mercerized	25.0	21.5
12	Tensile strength		
	(weft high-finished)		
	without ML, mercerized	Higher	Lower
		19.5	16
	with ML, mercerized	Higher	Lower
		24	19

The improved running properties obtained with rotor-spun yarns can only be secured, however, through optimization in warp preparation and sizing[390].

5.6.2 Warping

In carrying out comparisons between rotor- and ring-spun yarns, it is important to take into account the value of a well-prepared package for the warping process. Yarn breaks during warping are often claimed to be as commonly caused by spinning faults as by winding faults. Spinning faults are usually thick and thin places and slipped piecings, whereas the winding faults are the result of undersized packages running empty, loose ends and transfer tails tangling with running yarn, and pattern zones causing tension breaks. Tests carried out on cotton rotor-spun yarns of a commonly spun count of 56 tex, without rewinding or clearing, showed that a creeling set of 590 packages, i.e., a warp length of 37 600, gave a breakage rate of 21.18 per 10 000 km. Spinning faults accounted for 4.95 breaks per 10 000 km, the remainder being attributed to a poor build and to packages running empty prematurely because of having insufficient length. Where, in order to overcome premature emptying of packages, the calculated length to be warped is given a generous reserve, a significant amount of yarn can be left on the packages. Observations have shown that in such situations 15–20% of a full package can be left as remnants. Rewinding of the remnants to form new packages can be done, but, because the yarn will experience extra work, its properties, e.g., hairiness, can change sufficiently, albeit only slightly, to cause fabric faults. Thus the remnant yarns should not be reused. The cost-effectiveness of the rotor-spun yarn can therefore be unfavourably altered. It is recommended that, as a measure for strict quality control, rotor-spun yarns should be rewound and cleared before warping. This, however, may not be necessary if automatic piecing and doffing procedures are incorporated in the rotor-spinning line, provided that the machines can also demonstrate good and consistent package-building, i.e., in both package density and anti-patterning[390].

5.6.3 Sizing

It is well known that open-end-spun yarns have a lower tensile strength than ring-spun yarns. But, depending on the yarn fineness, the strength of rotor-spun yarns can be increased through sizing by 30–40%, i.e., an increase higher than that observed for conventional yarns. This effect is due to the different structure and the greater bulkiness of rotor-spun yarns. The sizing liquor penetrates even into the yarn core, and very good results are obtained with modified starch sizes[386]. In the sizing of open-end-spun yarns, the following factors must therefore be taken into account[391]:

- (*a*) the higher twist level of the yarn (size penetration);
- (*b*) the increased bulk;
- (*c*) the lower breaking strength;
- (*d*) the difference in hairiness; and
- (*e*) the increased elongation.

These factors will determine:

- (*a*) the required concentration of the sizing agent;
- (*b*) the optimum tension during sizing; and
- (*c*) the optimum nip pressure.

The concentration should be lower for rotor-spun yarns than for ring-spun yarns because of the compact arrangement of the fibre in the yarn cross-section and the difference in hairiness. If the same size concentration were used, the add-on for the rotor yarns would be 20–25% higher, resulting from the larger number of short and looped fibres projecting from the yarn. Moreover, because of the compactness of the yarn, size penetration would be different at this level of add-on, and an uneven coating of the yarn suface would result. End-breaks would therefore occur because the size could not penetrate the yarn to give the good flexibility required[391].

In order to improve the sizing of rotor-spun yarns, the nip pressure should be increased and the size viscosity reduced. The recommended tensions, given as a percentage of the rotor-spun-yarn breaking strength, are[391]:

in Zone 1 (from the bobbin to the nip roller in the size bath) 3–5%;
in Zone 2 (from the second nip rollers to the first drying drum) 5–7%;
in Zone 3 (from the drying drum to the chain area) 8–10%;
in Zone 4 (the warp beam) 18–20%.

Rotor-spun yarns are sensitive to overdrying, which happens when the machine is switched to low speeds and can result in an increase in breaks by 35–40%. The moisture content of the yarn should therefore be kept at 8.5–9.0%[391].

The quality of sizing is best determined by comparing the strength and extension of the sized and the unsized yarn. In one report, it is recommended that the breaking strength should be 20–25% higher than that for the unsized yarn and that the elongation should suffer no more than a 15% reduction; others have claimed up to a 20% reduction in elongation. The extension of the unsized yarn is the important factor; if this is too low, then the sized yarn will be unsuitable for being woven[391].

In a study involving the use of an SHKV 140 sizing machine for processing 25-tex cotton rotor-spun yarns, it was concluded that the optimum running conditions were[392]:

sizing speed: 80 m/min;
nip-roller pressure: 1.5 atm;
tension during warp beaming: 5–6 gf/yarn (49–59 mN/yarn);
temperature in size bath: 86°C.

The above conditions resulted in a drop in the number of loom breaks from 0.26 to 0.12 break/m.

Until recently, the structures of all rotor-spun yarns were regarded as being more or less the same, and it was generally assumed that these yarns absorbed 10% more size than ring-spun yarns. Experience has shown that the structure of rotor-spun yarns now produced varies a great deal, depending on the type of machine and spinning parameters used. For this reason, it can hardly be assumed that all currently commercially available rotor-spun yarns, with their varying structure, will take up size in the same manner and that, when sized, these yarns will all show a similar behaviour. Differences in the voluminosity of these sized yarns are sufficiently noticeable to have an influence on the appearance of the woven cloth. It is therefore inappropriate simply to regard rotor-spun yarns as a standard product, as is the case with conventional ring-spun yarns[393].

6. CONCLUSIONS

Rotor-spinning to-day is an economically viable process for the manufacture of short-staple yarns within the count range of 100–25 tex (6–24 N_e). Improved bearings have enabled rotor speeds as high as 70 000–80 000 r/min to be used for the production of such yarns, but machines running at these speeds will require automatic piecing, cleaning, and doffing.

The development of self-cleaning rotors, as well as improvements in opening-and-cleaning machinery, carding machines, and the beater section of the rotor-spinning machine, are reported to have helped in reducing the problem of rotor deposits, although it would also appear that spinners still keep a regular rotor-cleaning schedule. With regard to sliver cleanliness, a number of recommendations are cited, but the methods used to determine the various levels of trash in cotton slivers are either laborious or inaccurate. Research and development work in this area is still therefore necessary.

The importance of fibre–metal friction at high speeds is well recognized, particularly from the point of view of the wear of machine components and in the improvement of twist insertion by false-twisting at the doffing tube. However, there can be a deteriorating effect on yarn properties, depending on the count and fibre type (in particular, for man-made fibres), and it would appear that this has yet to be fully clarified. The yarn spinner needs to know, in no uncertain terms, when it is an advantage to use a ceramic, a highly polished smooth surface, or a roughened surface on his machine components.

Efforts have been made to extend the finer end of the count range of rotor-spun yarns, but with limited success. Not only are the technological problems difficult to solve, but, more importantly, the economics are also negatively biassed against the rotor-spinning process for the spinning of fine yarns. With more novel systems coming onto the market, e.g., friction spinning and air-jet spinning, aimed at the finer count range and producing yarn strengths more akin to those of ring-spun yarns, it is unlikely that rotor-spinning will make any significant progress in the finer count range.

Only limited progress has been made in the long-staple sector, principally because of two factors: the economic count limit and the wrapper-fibre problem. Again, more novel methods of spinning long-staple fibres (e.g., the DREF system, felted-yarn production, hollow-spindle and Siro spinning, and Duo spinning) may well displace any possible penetration of rotor-spinning in this sector.

ACKNOWLEDGEMENTS

The authors are grateful to Wira and the Shirley Institute for granting them access to their libraries and to Dr. R. Mashaly of the Textile Engineering Department at the University of Alexandria for his assistance.

The authors and publishers are also grateful for permission to reproduce in this issue several illustrations that have previously appeared elsewhere. Acknowledgement is made to *Textil-Praxis International* for Figures 1 and 2, to *Textile Manufacturer* for Figures 3–5, 7, and 39, to *Textile World* for Fig. 6, to *Textile Month* for Fig. 21, to *Indian Textile Journal* for Figures 34 and 37, to *Textil* for Figures 35 and 36, to the United Kingdom Patent Office for Figures 8–16, 18–20, 23, 25, 27, 32, 38, 40–43, 46, 47, and 50–52, and to the United States Patent Office for Figures 17, 22, 24, 26, 28–31, 44, 48, and 49.

Thanks are due to Messrs Schubert & Salzer Maschinenfabrik AG, who kindly supplied the illustration for the front cover.

REFERENCES

[1] V. A. Wakankar, R. J. Phatak, and R. Y. Churi. *Wool Woollens India*, 1981, Jan.–March, 33; *Text. Asia*, 1981, **12**, No. 10, 32.
[2] J. Ripken. *Melliand Textilber.*, 1980, **61**, 120 (*Eng. Edn*, 213).
[3] G. Egbers. *Text. Asia*, 1979, **10**, No. 11, 60.
[4] J. Gayler. *Textil-Praxis*, 1979, **34**, 891, (*Eng. Suppl.*, No. 8, II).
[5] B. Wulfhorst. *Textil-Praxis*, 1979, **34**, 639 (*Eng. Suppl.*, No. 6, II).
[6] J. Ripken. *Melliand Textilber.*, 1980, **61**, 120 (*Eng. Edn*, 213).
[7] *Chemiefasern/Textilindustrie*, 1978, **28/80**, 987 (E 164).
[8] *Text. World*, 1979, **129**, No. 9, 39.
[9] V. A. Wakankar, R. J. Phatak, and R. Y. Churi. *Wool Woollens India*, 1981, Jan–March, 33; *Text. Asia*, 1981, **12**, No. 10, 32.
[10] G. Worrall. *Text. Month*, 1978, May, 29.
[11] B. Wulfhorst. *Melliand Textilber.*, 1979, **60**, 983 (*Eng. Edn*, 994).
[12] B. Wulfhorst. *Text. Asia*, 1980, **11**, No. 4, 88.
[13] International Textile Manufacturers' Federation. 'International Textile Manufacturing', Vol. 1, 1978.
[14] International Textile Manufacturers' Federation. 'International Textile Manufacturing', Vol. 2, 1979.
[15] UMIST. *Text. Month*, 1979, Oct., 53.
[16] *Text. World*, 1979, **129**, No. 3, 51.
[17] P. R. Lord. *Text Industr.*, 1979, **143**, No. 8, 120.
[18] G. Worrall. *Text. Month*, 1978, June, 69.
[19] *Investa*, 1978, **9**, No. 3, July, 15.
[20] V. Kapek. *Tekstil. Prom.*, 1978, **38**, No. 5, 58.
[21] *Text. Month*, 1980, Feb., 59.
[22] V. Rohlena. *Investa*, 1979, **10**, No. 3, Sept., 6.
[23] F. Pešek. *Investa*, 1978, **9**, No. 3, July, 3.
[24] BD200RS Open-end-spinning machine, manufacturers' leaflet.
[25] *Text. Month*, 1979, June, 90.
[26] *Text. Mfr*, 1978, No. 4, 22.
[27] W. Schlafhorst & Co. *Text. Asia*, 1978, **9**, No. 5, 22.
[28] *Chemiefasern/Textilindustrie*, 1978, **28/80**, 987 (E 164).
[29] *Schlafhorst Inf.*, 1979, Aug., 5.
[30] B. Wulfhorst. *Chemiefasern/Textilindustrie*, 1980, **30/82**, 525 (E70).
[31] W. Andrew. *Int. Text. Mach.*, 1978, 26.
[32] *Chemiefasern/Textilindustrie*, 1978, **28/80**, 986 (E 164).
[33] *Text. Mfr*, 1978, No. 4, 22.
[34] F. Pešek. *Investa*, 1978, **9**, No. 3, July, 3.
[35] H. Stalder. *Int. Text. Bull., Spinning*, 1979, 155.
[36] *Text. Topics*, 1979, **7**, No. 7, March.
[37] *Textil-Praxis*, 1979, **34**, 15 (*Eng. Suppl.*, No. 1, II).
[38] W. Andrew. *Int. Text. Mach.*, 1978, 31.
[39] *Chemiefasern/Textilindustrie*, 1978, **28/80**, 987 (E 164).
[40] *Text. World*, 1979, **120**, No. 4, 44.
[41] *Text. Mfr*, 1978, No. 4, 22.
[42] *Textil-Praxis*, 1979, **34**, 225 (*Eng. Suppl.*, No. 3, V).
[43] *Text. Month*, 1979, Aug., 75.
[44] L. Bures. *Text. Asia*, 1980, **11**, No. 3, 83.
[45] *Investa*, 1980, **11**, No. 4, Sept., 14.
[46] V. Rohlena. *Chemiefasern/Textilindustrie*, 1980, **30/82**, 314 (E39).
[47] *Mod. Text.*, 1979, **60**, Feb., 17.
[48] J. Derichs. *Melliand Textilber.*, 1979, **60**, 539 (*Eng. Edn*, 532); *Indian Text. J.*, 1980, **90**, No. 9, June, 113.
[49] G. Worrall. *Text. Month*, 1978, May, 30.
[50] *Text. Month*, 1978, June, 31.
[51] G. Worrall. *Text. Month*, 1978, May, 29.
[52] Schubert & Salzer Maschinenfabrik AG. B.P. 1,523,053.
[53] Schubert & Salzer Maschinenfabrik AG. B.P. 1,523,271.
[54] N. Miyamoto, M. Shiraki, and K. Mitsuya. U.S.P. 4,254,612.
[55] T. Takeuchi, K. Ono, N. Furukawa, K. Sugiura, O. Suzuki, and T. Shimizu. U.S.P. 4,159,616.
[56] J. Ripka, V. Ohlidal, V. Vobornik, J. Elias, F. Jaros, C. Doublebsky, J. Junek, Z. Kotrba, M. Brozkova, and L. Lihtarova. Patent application GB 2,026,051A.
[57] Toyoda Jidoshokki Seisakusho KK. B.P. 1,582,172.
[58] A. Kobayashi, K. Chiba, N. Miyamoto, M. Shiraki, and N. Furukawa. U.S.P. 4,109,453.
[59] H. Stalder. U.S.P. 4,249,286.
[60] J. Ripka and V. Ohlidal. *Textil-Praxis*, 1978, **33**, 1186, 1344 (*Engl. Suppl.*, No. 10, VI; No. 11, XII).
[61] S. Rehm and K. Beizinger. U.S.P. 4,246,745.
[62] Karl-Heinz Schmolke. Patent application GB 2,055,916A.
[63] *Text. Month*, 1979, June, 90.
[64] *Text. World*, 1979, **129**, No. 4, 44.
[65] Hollingsworth GmbH. B.P. 1,514,123.
[66] W. Schaeffler, G. Schaeffler, and W. Donath. Patent application GB 2,044,808A.
[67] J. Shaw and B. Ellingham. B.P. 1,517,273.

[68] W. R. Stewart and D. B. Stewart. B.P. 1,510,623.
[69] J. Simpson and M. F. Murray. *Text. Res J.*, 1979, **49**, 506.
[70] H. Heinen. Patent application GB 2,045,822A.
[71] Platt Saco Lowell Ltd. B.P. 1,587,821.
[72] B. Kveton. *Investa*, 1980, **11**, No. 4, Sept., 14.
[73] N. Miyamoto, M. Shiraki, and K. Mitsuya. Patent application GB 2,038,895A.
[74] H. Stalder. *Int. Text. Bull., Spinning*, 1979, 155.
[75] D. A. Bowen. *Text. Industr.*, 1980, **144**, No. 10, 66.
[76] M. Graf, P. Schwengeler, and H. Stalder. Patent application GB 2,021,159A.
[77] A. Horikawa, O. Yaida, and M. Niida. *J. Text. Mach. Soc. Japan*, 1980, **33**, No. 7, T78.
[78] J. Le Chatelier. Patent application GB 2,017,164A.
[79] F. A. Aschenbrenner and W. V. Wright. Patent application GB 2,027,064A.
[80] F. A. Aschenbrenner and W. V. Wright. U.S.P. 4,170,866.
[81] J. Ripka and V. Ohlidal. *Textil-Praxis*, 1978, **33**, 1186, 1344 (*Eng. Suppl.*, No. 10, VI; No. 11, XII).
[82] J. Ripka and V. Ohlidal. *Textil-Praxis*, 1979, **34**, 120, (*Eng. Suppl.*, No. 2, VI; No. 5, XII).
[83] S. Shenmei, Q. Zhimin, and others. *Shanghai Fangzhi Gongxueyuan Xusbao*, 1980, **6**, No. 2, 55.
[84] P. Grosberg and K. H. Ho. *Appl. Polymer Symp.*, 1977, No. 31, 83.
[85] W. Kampen, J. Lünenschloss, T. T. Phoa, and D. Rossbach. *Int. Text. Bull., Spinning*, 1979, 373.
[86] P. R. Lord and T. Giorgis. 'Book of Papers for the 17th Canadian Textile Seminar', Textile Technical Federation of Canada, Montreal, Canada, 1980, p. 51.
[87] P. R. Lord. *Text. Month*, 1980, Dec., 45.
[88] Feldmühle AG. B.P. 1,568,070.
[89] J. P. van der Merwe and D. P. Veldsman. SAWTRI Technical Report No. 389, 1978.
[90] J. Havel, V. Vobornik, J. Ripka, F. Jaros, F. Hortlik, A. Planansky, and B. Rehackova. U.S.P. 4,110,961.
[91] Výzkumny Ústav Bavlnářský. B.P. 1,536,078.
[92] F. Duba. U.S.P. 4,166,354.
[93] J. Le Chatelier and M. Kueny. U.S.P. 4,258,541.
[94] J. Le Chatelier and M. Kueny. Patent application GB 2,017,167A.
[95] SKF Kugellagerfabriken GmbH. B.P. 1,519,705.
[96] J. Whiteley. U.S.P. 4,170,102.
[97] SKF Kugellagerfabriken GmbH. B.P. 1,540,440.
[98] F. Stahlecker and H. Stahlecker. U.S.P. 4,112,659.
[99] Maschinenfabrik Rieter AG. B.P. 1,529,550.
[100] P. Schwengeler. U.S.P. 4,176,512.
[101] E. Braun and E. Bock. U.S.P. 4,184,315.
[102] A. Abduganiev, V. N. Tikhonov, G. N. Shlykov, V. I. Zhestkov, T. P. Krjuk, V. M. Mukhin, and J. N. Tikhonov. Patent application GB 2,055,405A.
[103] F. Stahlecker and H. Stahlecker. U.S.P. 4,098,065.
[104] Platt Saco Lowell Ltd. B.P. 1,577,953.
[105] G. Fusaroll. U.S.P. 4,193,254.
[106] G. C. Anderson and J. W. B. Clayton, U.S.P. 4,122,655.
[107] J. W. B. Clayton and D. O. Clough. U.S.P. 4,204,391.
[108] Feldmühle AG. B.P. 1,568,070.
[109] Société Anonyme des Ateliers Houget Duesberg Bosson. B.P. 1,556,475.
[110] Schubert & Salzer Maschinenfabrik AG. B.P. 1,529,404.
[111] D. Cormack, P. Grosberg, and K. H. Ho. *J. Text. Inst.*, 1979, **70**, 380.
[112] A. Kobayashi, K. Chiba, N. Miyamoto, M. Shiraki, and N. Furukawa. U.S.P. 4,109,452.
[113] F. Stahlecker and H. Stahlecker. U.S.P. 4,186,548.
[114] Schubert & Salzer Maschinenfabrik AG. B.P. 1,563,985.
[115] W. Schaeffler, G. Schaeffler, and W. Donath. Patent application GB 2,044,808A.
[116] Kabushiki Kaishanegish KK. B.P. 1,533,709.
[117] P. R. Lord. *J. Text. Inst.*, 1980, **71**, 221.
[118] J. Shaw, J. Whiteley, and S. Martin. U.S.P. 4,167,846.
[119] W. Herbert, W. Kunz, and K. Pimiskern. U.S.P. 4,193,253.
[120] R. V. Wright and R. E. Carter. U.S.P. 4,216,644.
[121] V. Kapek. *Tekstil. Prom.*, 1978, **38**, No. 5, 58.
[122] H. Wehde and G. Quandt. *Melliand Textilber.*, 1978, **59**, 705.
[123] Teldix GmbH. B.P. 1,566,040.
[124] M. Chrtek, J. Gabler, F. Tuma, K. Kasparek, and J. Blasko. U.S.P. 4,112,663.
[125] Teldix GmbH. B.P. 1,587,180.
[126] A. Kobayashi, K. Chiba, N. Miyamoto, M. Shiraki, and N. Furukawa. U.S.P. 4,109,452.
[127] N. Miyamoto, M. Shiraki, and K. Mitsuya. U.S.P. 4,254,614.
[128] F. Pešek. *Investa*, 1978, **9**, No. 3, July, 3.
[129] Maschinenfabrik Rieter AG. B.P. 1,545,661.
[130] F. Stahlecker and H. Stahlecker. U.S.P. 4,116,505.
[131] H. R. Victor and J. Schmidt in Seventh International Gas Bearing Symposium, 1976.
[132] V. Rohlena. *Chemiefasern/Textilindustrie*, 1980, **30/82**, 314 (E 39).
[133] Johannes Heidenhain GmbH. B.P. 1,581,565.
[134] SKF Kugellagerfabriken GmbH. B.P. 1,555,356.
[135] R. S. Maynard and J. Schaepers in Meeting of Rochdale & District Textile Works Managers' Association, 16 March, 1981.

[136] Société Alsacienne de Constructions Mécaniques de Mulhouse (SACM). *Textil-Praxis*, 1979, **34**, 255.
[137] I. Sharieff. *J. Text. Assoc.*, 1979, **40**, 11.
[138] F. Stahlecker and H. Stahlecker. B.P. 1,512,448.
[139] V. Rohlena. *Chemiefasern/Textilindustrie*, 1980, **30/82**, 314 (E 39).
[140] F. Stahlecker and H. Stahlecker. U.S.P. 4,186,548.
[141] Schubert & Salzer Maschinenfabrik AG. B.P. 1,563,985.
[142] W. Schaeffler, G. Schaeffler, and W. Donath. Patent application GB 2,044,808A.
[143] A. Kobayashi, K. Chiba, N. Miyamoto, M. Shiraki, and N. Furukawa. U.S.P. 4,149,365.
[144] G. Kohler, H. W. Munkel, H. Pohl, W. Sommer, and G. Wendel. U.S.P. 4,084,860.
[145] H. Munnich and H. Glockner. U.S.P. 4,167,845.
[146] W. Schaeffler, G. Schaeffler, and W. Donath. Patent application GB 2,044,808A.
[147] SKF Kugellagerfabriken GmbH. B.P. 1,556,726.
[148] *Text. Month*, 1978, Aug., 59.
[149] K. Aeppli. U.S.P. 4,007,457.
[150] P. Artzt, G. Egbers, R. Guse, and S. Tabibi. U.S.P. 4,246,748.
[151] Schubert & Salzer Maschinenfabrik AG. B.P. 1,521,951.
[152] *Text. Month*, 1978, Aug., 59.
[153] S. Peyer. B.P. 1,563,830.
[154] *Chemiefasern/Textilindustrie*, 1978, **28/80**, 987 (E 164).
[155] Schubert & Salzer Maschinenfabrik AG. B.P. 1,511,764.
[156] *Canad. Text. J.*, 1978, **95**, No. 11, 84.
[157] H. Wehde, F. Schumann, and B. Wulfhorst. U.S.P. 4,209,778.
[158] H. Wehde. U.S.P. 4,238,789.
[159] Teldix GmbH. B.P. 1,581,297.
[160] Teldix GmbH. B.P. 1,579,085.
[161] H. Wehde, B. Wulfhorst, and F. Schumann. U.S.P. 4,242,860.
[162] H. Wehde, B. Wulfhorst, and F. Schumann. Patent application GB 2,010,344A.
[163] F. Stahlecker and H. Stahlecker. U.S.P. 4,084,398.
[164] Platt Saco Lowell Ltd. U.S.P. 4,228,642.
[165] Y. Suzuki, K. Sugiura, O. Suzuki, and I. Tashiro. U.S.P. 4,112,661.
[166] Toyoda Jidoshokki Seisakusho KK, O. Suzuki, T. Yochizawa, and Y. Yoshida. Patent application GB 2,050,439A.
[167] Y. Yoshida, O. Suzuki, K. Onoue, and K. Seiki. Patent application GB 2,044,807A.
[168] F. Stahlecker and H. Stahlecker. B.P. 1,530,919.
[169] J. Dykast, K. Mikulecky, and M. Tyl. Patent application GB 2,019,451A.
[170] T. Takeuchi, K. Ono, N. Furukawa, K. Sugiura, O. Suzuki, and T. Shimizu. U.S.P. 4,163,358.
[171] Platt Saco Lowell Ltd. B.P. 1,548,004.
[172] Y. Yoshida, O. Suzuki, and K. Onoue. U.S.P. 4,109,450.
[173] Maschinenfabrik Rieter AG. B.P. 1,526,506.
[174] E. Furrer. U.S.P. 4,094,133.
[175] J. Derichs. *Melliand Textilber.*, 1979, **60**, 539 (*Eng. Edn*, 532).
[176] J. Derichs. *Indian Text. J.*, 1980, **90**, No. 9, June, 113.
[177] Institut für Textiltechnik, Reutlingen. *Textil-Praxis*, 1981, **36**, 129 (*Eng. Suppl.*, No. 2, IV).
[178] J. Elias and K. Mikulecky. *Textil*, 1979, **34**, 367.
[179] Toyoda Jidoshokki Seisakusho KK, T. Yoshizawa, O. Suzuki, and Y. Yoshida. Patent application GB 2,052,573A.
[180] F. Stahlecker and H. Stahlecker. U.S.P. 1,509,955.
[181] W. Reiners Verwaltungs GmbH. B.P. 1,586,806.
[182] K. Mikulecky, M. Tyl, J. Janousek, F. Burysek, S. Skoda, and S. Esner. U.S.P. 4,104,854.
[183] F. Stahlecker and H. Stahlecker. B.P. 1,527,052.
[184] H. Stahlecker and H. Schulz. U.S.P. 4,222,225.
[185] F. Stahlecker and H. Stahlecker. U.S.P. Re 30 167.
[186] Battelle Memorial Institute. B.P. 1,551,205.
[187] T. Honjo. U.S.P. 4,142,358.
[188] Battelle Memorial Institute. U.S.P. 4,150,532.
[189] W. Reiners Verwaltungs GmbH. B.P. 1,581,792.
[190] H. Kamp. U.S.P. 4,145,867.
[191] J. Derichs and H. Raasch. Patent application GB 2,035,395A.
[192] F. Stahlecker and H. Stahlecker. U.S.P. 4,107,957.
[193] A. Smith. U.S.P. 4,221,110.
[194] K. Mikulecky, J. Elias, F. Burysek, S. Esner, S. Skoda, M. Tyl, and J. Janousek. U.S.P. 4,246,749.
[195] K. Mikulecky, J. Elias, F. Burysek, S. Esner, S. Skoda, M. Tyl, and J. Janousek. Patent application GB 2,019,452A.
[196] F. Eckhardt. U.S.P. 4,114,356.
[197] W. Reiners Verwaltungs GmbH. B.P. 1,552,050.
[198] J. Derichs. U.S.P. 4,150,530.
[199] W. Reiners Berwaltungs GmbH. B.P. 1,532,852.
[200] J. Derichs, H. Raasch, L. Neuhaus, D. Langheinrich, H. Schlosser, and E. Baltsch. U.S.P. 4,102,116.
[201] F. Stahlecker and H. Stahlecker. U.S.P. 4,172,357.
[202] T. Honjo. U.S.P. 4,163,359.
[203] F. Stahlecker and H. Stahlecker. U.S.P. Re 30 201.
[204] H. Stahlecker and F. Stahlecker. U.S.P. 4,175,370.
[205] W. Reiners Verwaltungs GmbH. B.P. 1,566,518.
[206] O. Suzuki, S. Ueda, and I. Tashiro. U.S.P. 4,100,722.

[207] C. R. Martin, P. B. Tarbox, and S. W. Yates. U.S.P. 4,248,037.
[208] J. Elias and K. Mikulecky. Patent application GB 2,028,284A.
[209] *Int. Text. Bull., Spinning*, 1979, 349.
[210] F. Stahlecker and H. Stahlecker. U.S.P. 4,178,749.
[211] K. Tsuzuki, K. Motobayashi, K. Watanabe, Y. Kito, and S. Seko. U.S.P. 4,249,369.
[212] P. Artzt. *Textil-Praxis*, 1978, **33,** 678 (*Eng. Suppl.*, VII).
[213] H. Hirai and K. Tsubata. U.S.P. 4,110,960.
[214] H. Raasch and H. Grecksch. U.S.P. 4,120,140.
[215] F. Stahlecker. U.S.P. 4,089,155.
[216] E. Braun, E. Bock, K. Hanschuch, and E. Schuller. Patent application GB 2,017,169A.
[217] W. Reiners Verwaltungs GmbH. B.P. 1,551,288.
[218] H. Stahlecker and F. Stahlecker. U.S.P. 4,155,217.
[219] H. Stahlecker and F. Stahlecker. U.S.P. 4,125,991.
[220] H. Stahlecker and F. Stahlecker. U.S.P. 4,135,354.
[221] Výzkumny Ústav Bavlnářský. B.P. 1,577,845.
[222] M. Chrtek, F. Tuma, J. Gabler, K. Kasparek, and J. Blasko. U.S.P. 4,166,356.
[223] E. Bock, E. Braun, and B. Wulfhorst. U.S.P. 4,211,063.
[224] Y. Yamasa, K. Kamiya, I. Katayama, K. Motobayashi, and Y. Yonemura. U.S.P. 4,109,451.
[225] Nuova San Giorgio SpA. B.P. 1,543,065.
[226] F. Stahlecker. U.S.P. 4,098,066.
[227] F. Stahlecker and H. Stahlecker. B.P. 1,519,259.
[228] L. Bures. *Investa*, 1979, **10,** No. 1, 2.
[229] L. Bures. *Canad. Text. J.*, 1979, **96,** No. 11, 54.
[230] F. Stahlecker and H. Stahlecker. U.S.P. 4,178,749.
[231] Barber-Colman Co. *Text. Inst. Industr.*, 1980, **18,** 120.
[232] T. Miyazaki, T. Kato, Y. Suzuki, and S. Ueda. U.S.P. 4,118,920.
[233] K. Vlcek, Z. Pacakova, B. Jirka, B. Cesenek, and K. Jindra. U.S.P. 4,088,226.
[234] F. Stahlecker. H. Stahlecker, H. Kamp, and H. Raasch. U.S.P. 4,125,990.
[235] R. Nield and E. F. Abadeer. *J. Text. Inst.*, 1979, **70,** 286.
[236] R. Nield and E. F. Abadeer. *J. Text. Inst.*, 1979, **70,** 281.
[237] P. R. Lord. *J. Text. Inst.*, 1980, **71,** 221.
[238] *Text. Asia*, 1979, **10,** No. 6, 71.
[239] L. C. Tortosa, T. Phoa, and D. Rossbach. *Int. Text. Bull., Spinning*, 1978, 29.
[240] R. Nield and E. F. Abadeer. *J. Text. Inst.*, 1979, **70,** 281.
[241] R. F. Huber, *Wool Woollens India*, 1981, Jan.–March, 13; *Text. Asia*, 1981, **12,** No. 6, 41.
[242] A. Schenek, P. Artzt, and R. Ali. *Textil-Praxis*, 1980, **35,** 397 (*Eng. Suppl.*, No. 4, II).
[243] K. D. Langley and H. Haasma. *Text. Res. J.*, 1979, **49,** 455.
[244] R. Nield. *J. Text. Inst.*, 1980, **71,** 221.
[245] Texas Tech University. *Text. Topics*, 1978, **7,** No. 2, Oct.
[246] P. R. Lord. *Text. Month*, 1980, Dec., 45.
[247] R. Nield and E. F. Abadeer. *J. Text. Inst.*, 1979, **70,** 371.
[248] N. Miyamoto. Patent application GB 2,017,170A.
[249] N. Miyamoto. U.S.P. 4,237,682.
[250] L. C. Tortosa, T. Phoa, and D. Rossbach. *Int. Text. Bull., Spinning*, 1978, 29.
[251] R. F. Huber. *Wool Woollens India*, 1981, Jan.–March, 13; *Text. Asia*, 1981, **12,** No. 6. 41.
[252] A. Schenek, P. Artzt, and R. Ali. *Textil-Praxis*, 1980, **35,** 397 (*Eng. Suppl.*, No. 4, II).
[253] *Text. World*, 1979, **129,** No. 3, 51.
[254] J. D. Towery and R. V. Baker. *Text. Res. J.*, 1979, **49,** 127.
[255] A. C. Griffin and J. D. Bargeron. Marketing Research Report No. 1110, United States Department of Agriculture, Washington, D.C., 1980.
[256] *Text. Asia*, 1979, **10,** No. 6, 71.
[257] J. Simpson. *Text. Res. J.*, 1980, **50,** 507.
[258] R. F. Huber. *Wool Woollens India*, 1981, Jan.–March, 13; *Text. Asia*, 1981, **12,** No. 6, 41.
[259] J. Simpson. *Amer. Text.: Rep./Bull. Edn*, 1978, **AT7,** No. 9, 46.
[260] S. K. Nerurkar and G. D. Chitnis. *Text. Mach. Accessories & Stores*, 1979, **15,** No. 4, July–Aug., 7.
[261] J. D. Spencer and H. Taylor. *SAWTRI Bull.*, 1979, **13,** No. 3, Sept., 16.
[262] University of Manchester Institute of Science and Technology. *Text. Month*, 1979, Oct., 53.
[263] S. D. Supanekar and S. K. Nerurkar. *Text. Res. J.*, 1979, **49,** 26.
[264] *Text. Asia*, 1979, **10,** No. 6, 71.
[265] A. M. Avilov and R. F. Krakhmaleva. *Tekstil. Prom.*, 1979, **39,** No. 5, 35.
[266] J. P. van der Merwe, H. Taylor, and D. P. Veldsman. SAWTRI Technical Report No. 397, 1978.
[267] H. Taylor and J. D. Spencer. *SAWTRI Bull.*, 1978, **12,** June, 14.
[268] *Text. Mfr*, 1978, No. 4, 22.
[269] J. M. Grover. *J. Text. Assoc.*, 1979, **40,** No. 2, 45.
[270] R. F. Huber. *Wool Woollens India*, 1981, Jan.–March, 13; *Text. Asia*, 1981, **12,** No. 6, 41.
[271] U. S. Ochirov. *Tekhnol. Tekstil. Prom.*, 1980, No. 2 (134), 88.
[272] Texas Tech University. *Text. Topics*, 1978, **6,** No. 8, April.
[273] R. Wildbolz. *Chemiefasern/Textilindustrie*, 1978, **28/80,** 980 (E 175).
[274] Texas Tech University. *Text. Topics*, 1978, **6,** No. 9, May.
[275] F. M. Plekhanov. *Tekstil. Prom.*, 1979, **39,** No. 6, 34.
[276] F. Pešek. *Investa*, 1978, **9,** No. 3, July, 3.

[277] Toyoda Jidoshokki Seisakusho KK, K. Onoue, T. Katoh, Y. Yoshida, and K. Seiki. Patent application GB 2,049,750A.
[278] Toyoda Jidoshokki Seisakusho KK, K. Onoue, T. Katoh, Y. Yoshida, and K. Seiki. Patent application GB 2,046,320A.
[279] P. Artzt, R. Hehl, G. Egbers, and A. Schenek. U.S.P. 4,201,037.
[280] Platt Saco Lowell Ltd. B.P. 1,551,068.
[281] T. Miyazaki, M. Shiraki, and K. Mitsuya. U.S.P. 4,204,393.
[282] Parks-Cramer Ltd. B.P. 1,515,055.
[283] H. V. Ditshuizen, F. Schumann, G. Goldammer, and R. Glaser. U.S.P. 4,162,556.
[284] Zinser Textilmaschinen GmbH. B.P. 1,518,629.
[285] Schubert & Salzer Maschinenfabrik AG. B.P. 1,526,595.
[286] M. Vecera and J. Skala. U.S.P. 4,249,370.
[287] R. Nield and E. F. Abadeer. *J. Text. Inst.*, 1979, **70**, 367.
[288] R. Nield and E. F. Abadeer. *J. Text. Inst.*, 1979, **70**, 371.
[289] *Text. Asia*, 1979, **10**, No. 6, 71.
[290] Toyoda Jidoshokki Seisakusho KK, K. Seiki, T. Katoh, and Y. Yoshida. Patent application GB 2,049,743A.
[291] N. Miyamoto. Patent application GB 2,017,170A.
[292] Texas Tech University. *Text. Topics*, 1978, **6**, No. 11.
[293] Texas Tech University. *Text. Topics*, 1979, **7**, No. 9, May.
[294] V. N. Tikhonov, G. N. Shlykov, V. I. Zhestkov, G. V. Zhigalov, V. M. Mukhin, and V. M. Dyachkov. U.S.P. 4,245,459.
[295] Maschinenfabrik Rieter AG. B.P. 1,524,299.
[296] J. Le Chatelier. Patent application GB 2,020,319A.
[297] J. Le Chatelier. U.S.P. 4,241,572.
[298] M. F. Murray and C. L. Folk. *Text. Res. J.*, 1979, **49**, 140.
[299] Toyoda Jidoshokki Seisakusho KK, K. Onoue, T. Katoh, Y. Yoshida, and K. Seiki. GB 2,046,320A.
[300] G. L. Louis. *Text. Res. J.*, 1980, **50**, 641.
[301] R. A. Ali, P. Artzt, H. Muller, A. Schenek, and K. Lehmann. GB 2,054,671A.
[302] H. Staufert and F. Stahlecker. U.S.P. 4,245,460.
[303] Brown Boveri & Co. Ltd and Y. H. Dschen. Patent application GB 2,004,307A.
[304] Elitex. BP 1,541,491.
[305] Brown Boveri & Co. Ltd and Y. H. Dschen. U.S.P. 4,242,858.
[306] *Text. World*, 1979, **129**, No. 9, 39.
[307] B. Wulfhorst. *Melliand Textilber.*, 1979, **60**, 983 (*Eng. Edn*, 994).
[308] B. Wulfhorst. *Text. Asia*, 1980, **11**, No. 4, 80.
[309] H. Landwehrkamp. *Melliand Textilber.*, 1979, **60**, 912 (*Eng. Edn.*, 919).
[310] J. Prihoda and J. Berankova. *Investa*, 1979, **10**, No. 1, 9.
[311] H. Stalder. *Int. Text. Bull., Spinning*, 1979, 155.
[312] J. Simpson and M. F. Murray. *Text. Res. J.*, 1978, **48**, 270.
[313] A. K. Sengupta, B. Dutta, and P. Radhakrishnaiah. *Text. Res. J.*, 1981, **51**, 70.
[314] A. K. Sengupta, B. Dutta, and P. Radhakrishnaiah. *Text. Res. J.*, 1980, **50**, 228.
[315] K. N. Seshan, K. P. R. Pillay, T. V. Ratnam, and S. Govindarajan in 'Cotton in a Competitive World' (edited by P. W. Harrison), the Textile Institute, Manchester, 1979, p. 202.
[316] H. H. Perkins and J. D. Bargerson. Marketing Research Report No. 1094, United States Department of Agriculture, Washington, D.C., 1978.
[317] J. Prihoda and J. Berankova. *Investa*, 1979, **10**, No. 1, 9.
[318] H. Landwehrkamp. *Melliand Textilber.*, 1979, **60**, 912 (*Eng. Edn*, 919).
[319] K. R. Salhotra. *J. Text. Assoc.*, 1980, **41**, 115.
[320] A. Barella and J. P. Vigo. *J. Text. Inst.*, 1979, **70**, 500.
[321] E. Gee. *J. Text. Inst.*, 1979, **70**, 500.
[322] A. Barella and J. P. Vigo. *J. Text. Inst.*, 1978, **69**, 342.
[323] A. Barella and J. P. Vigo. *J. Text. Inst.*, 1978, **69**, 336.
[324] *Text. Month*, 1979, Aug., 66.
[325] *Text. World*, 1979, **129**, No. 9, 39.
[326] B. Wulfhorst. *Melliand Textilber.*, 1979, **60**, 983 (*Eng. Edn*, 994).
[327] Texas Tech University. *Text. Topics*, 1979, **8**, No. 3, Nov.
[328] Texas Tech University. *Text. Topics*, 1979, **7**, No. 7, March.
[329] Texas Tech University. *Text. Topics*, 1979, **7**, No. 12, Aug.
[330] J. Simpson and M. A. Patureau. *Text. Res. J.*, 1979, **49**, 468.
[331] *Text. Month*, 1979, Aug., 66.
[332] Texas Tech University. *Text. Topics*, 1979, **8**, No. 2, Oct.
[333] A. Barella and J. P. Vigo. *J. Text. Inst.*, 1980, **71**, 195.
[334] O. M. Nikiforov. *Tekhnol. Tekstil. Prom.*, 1978, No. 1 (121), 36.
[335] Texas Tech University. *Text. Topics*, 1979, **7**, No. 11, July.
[336] Platt Saco Lowell Ltd. B.P. 1,565,949.
[337] James Mackie & Sons Ltd. B.P. 1,569,123.
[338] G. Husges, E. Schuller, R. Karl, and E. Grimm. U.S.P. 4,223,517.
[339] J. D. Towery. *Text. Industr.*, 1979, **143**, No. 9, 90.
[340] A. Barella and J. P. Vigo. *J. Text. Inst.*, 1980, **71**, 324.
[341] J. Stary and A. Kubicek. *Investa*, 1978, **9**, No. 3, July, 10.
[342] J. Stary and A. Kubicek. *Canad. Text. J.*, 1979, **96**, No. 2, 46.

[343] H. Landwehrkamp. *Melliand Textilber.*, 1979, **60**, 825 (*Eng. Edn*, 819).
[344] H. Landwehrkamp. *Text. Asia*, 1980, **11**, No. 1, 88.
[345] H. Landwehrkamp. *Chemiefasern/Textilindustrie*, 1979, **29/81**, 973 (E 132).
[346] D. H. Darden. *Text. World*, 1980, **130**, No. 5, 70.
[347] F. S. Looney. *Text. World*, 1978, **128**, No. 12, 40.
[348] H. Landwehrkamp. *Melliand Textilber.*, 1979, **60**, 825 (*Eng. Edn*, 819).
[349] A. Naik and F. Lopez-Amo, in 'Cotton in a Competitive World' (edited by P. W. Harrison), the Textile Institute, Manchester, 1979, p. 184.
[350] W. S. Schmidt and U. P. Dorsch. Patent application GB 2,022,162A.
[351] J. Vasatko, J. Stary, S. Kroulik, and V. Hladik. *Textil*, 1976, **31**, 405; *Melliand Textilber.*, 1978, **59**, 710 (*Eng. Edn*, 682).
[352] P. Lennox-Kerr. *Text. World*, 1979, **129**, No. 4, 40.
[353] A. Barella, J. P. Vigo, and A. M. Manich. *J. Text. Inst.*, 1980, **71**, 242.
[354] A. Barella and J. P. Vigo. *J. Text. Inst.*, 1980, **71**, 189.
[355] J. P. Vigo and A. Barella. *Text. Res. J.*, 1981, **51**, 34.
[356] B. A. Bakulin and A. P. Litvinova. *Tekstil. Prom.*, 1979, **39**, No. 8, 38.
[357] H. Landwehrkamp. *Melliand Textilber.*, 1979, **60**, 825 (*Eng. Edn.*, 819).
[358] A. Barella, J. P. Vigo, J. M. Tura, and L. Castro. *Textil-Praxis*, 1979, **34**, 1341 (*Eng. Suppl.*, No. 10, XVI).
[359] B. Schonung. *Textil-Praxis*, 1980, **35**, 1190 (*Eng. Suppl.*, No. 10, VI).
[360] K. Lumpp. *Textil-Praxis*, 1980, **35**, 679 (*Eng. Suppl.*, No. 6, II).
[361] A. Barella and J. P. Vigo. *Text. Res. J.*, 1978, **48**, 473.
[362] A. Barella, J. P. Vigo, and A. M. Manich. *Text. Inst. Industr.*, 1980, **18**, 238.
[363] D. H. Darden. *Text. World*, 1980, **130**, No. 5, 70.
[364] G. I. Muratova. *Tekhnol. Tekstil. Prom.*, 1979, No. 2 (128), 33.
[365] P. Artzt and H. Muller. *Chemiefasern/Textilindustrie*, 1979, **29/81**, 529 (E 78).
[366] G. Meinck and A. Schuren. *Melliand Textilber.*, 1980, **61**, 492 (*Eng. Edn*, 661).
[367] K. I. Koritskiĭ. *Tekstil. Prom.*, 1979, **39**, No. 6, 32.
[368] V. M. Oganesyan, S. A. Minasyan, S. S. Astoyan, and G. S. Pailevanyan. *Tekhnol. Tekstil. Prom.*, 1980, No. 2 (134), 36.
[369] K. K. Akhmedov and Y. B. Kapralov. *Tekstil. Prom.*, 1979, **39**, No. 12, 28.
[370] H. Landwehrkamp. *Text. Res. J.*, 1979, **49**, 137.
[371] B. Schonung. *Textil-Praxis*, 1980, **35**, 1291 (*Eng. Suppl.*, No. 11, II).
[372] G. Mazingue. *Melliand Textilber.*, 1981, **62**, 7, (*Eng. Edn*, 2).
[373] J. D. Spencer and H. Taylor. *SAWTRI Bull.*, 1978, **12**, No. 3, 31.
[374] J. D. Spencer and H. Taylor. *SAWTRI Bull.*, 1978, **12**, No. 4, 14.
[375] J. Lünenschloss and W. Kampen. *Melliand Textilber.*, 1980, **61**, 769 (*Eng. Edn*, 1214).
[376] *Investa*, 1978, **9**, No. 3, July, 14.
[377] H. Landwehrkamp. *Text. Res. J.*, 1979, **49**, 137.
[378] J. Shimizu, W. Ishibashi, and Y. N. Wang. *Proc. Int. Wool Text. Res. Conf. Aachen*, 1975; published in *Schriftenreihe Deutsches Wollforschungsinstitut an der Technischen Hochschule Aachen*, 1976, IV–266.
[379] D. P. Veldsman and H. Taylor. SAWTRI Technical Report No. 412, 1978.
[380] E. H. Pittman. U.S.P. 4,218,868.
[381] Milliken Research Corporation and E. H. Pittman. Patent application GB 2,046,322A.
[382] H. Edagawa, T. Fujita, and Y. Llesugi. Patent application GB 2,003,528A.
[383] R. Nield and A. R. A. Ali. *J. Text. Inst.*, 1977, **68**, 223.
[384] *Man-made Text. India*, 1978, 573.
[385] K. Nick. Sulzer Information.
[386] L. Skrbek. *Investa*, 1980, **11**, No. 3, Sept., 7.
[387] A. Biederman. *Investa*, 1980, **11**, No. 3, Sept., 2.
[388] K. Nick. *Text. Asia*, 1979, **10**, No. 2, 24.
[389] G. I. Muratova. *Tekhnol. Tekstil. Prom.*, 1979, No. 2 (128) 33.
[390] *Schlafhorst Inf.*, 1979, Aug.
[391] V. I. Shurupov. *Tekstil. Prom.*, 1980, **40**, No. 4, 38.
[392] B. A. Bakulin and G. K. Popova. *Tekhnol. Tekstil. Prom.*, 1978, No. 5 (125), 65.
[393] R. A. Schutz, P. E. Exbrayat, and D. Carriere. *Textil-Praxis*, 1980, **35**, 264 (*Eng. Suppl.*, No. 3, II).

NAME INDEX*

---

* The Name and Subject Indexes, which were prepared by the author, have been compiled in relation to the bibliographical references and not to the page numbers.

SUBJECT INDEX*

* See footnote to first page of Name Index.